YES, I AM THE SURGEON

YES, I AM THE SURGEON

LESSONS ON PERSEVERANCE IN A WORLD THAT TELLS YOU NO

LATTISHA LATOYAH
BILBREW, MD

Yes, I Am the Surgeon
Lessons on Perseverance in a World That Tells You No

FIRST EDITION

ISBN 978-1-5445-3946-1 Hardcover
978-1-5445-3945-4 Paperback
978-1-5445-3944-7 Ebook
978-1-5445-3947-8 Audiobook

This book is dedicated to

The Windrush Generation.

To those who left their homes to rebuild and

establish a greater future for their

children and grandchildren.

George Adolphus

Joyce Linda

Martin Constantine

Beryl Agatha

CONTENTS

INTRODUCTION

My earliest career aspiration was to be a hairdresser. Those aspirations were redirected at the age of four, when I witnessed something that would change my entire trajectory.

My maternal grandmother, my Nanny, was always sick. She was also headstrong. You'll learn more about her in the next chapter. Nanny was routinely hospitalized, usually from the effects of treatable issues, like hypertension. I often sat with her when she was hospitalized; although the hospital can be a source of fear for many people, I never felt afraid sitting beside her while she lay bedridden and connected to a variety of beeping machines. I enjoyed the hospital—its clean white hallways, the bustling around the nurses' station. I even loved, and still do, the antiseptic *smell* of it.

One day in particular, my parents and my sister had wandered somewhere, leaving me alone with Nanny in her semi-private room. A staff member—possibly a nurse, doctor, or a tech—swung around from the sheet separating my grandmother from her hospital roommate. She was ready to administer my grandmother's medication.

The woman was very curt, saying, "Take your medicine," and handing her a small paper cup. She didn't ask how my grandmother was feeling, nor did she explain what the medication was supposed to do or ask if she would like a sip of water first.

Nanny looked over at me, speaking volumes with her eyes—the way many older Jamaican women can relay an entire story by merely raising an eyebrow. I knew she was telling me, without saying a word, *Watch what I am about to do*. Dutifully, my grandmother placed the pills under her tongue and waited for the healthcare professional to walk away. Then, Nanny motioned me to come closer, and I wandered over to the nightstand next to her bed, watching as she opened the drawer and spat out all the pills.

When I peered into the drawer, I saw it was holding piles of them. Staring into that drawer of oval white pills, I saw many unknowns. I did not know the pharmacological makeup of the pills—nothing about the dosage, side effects, or half-lives. I did not fully comprehend the insincerity of the healthcare worker's visit to her bedside. Yet, even at a young age, the feeling that was branded into my memory—the feeling that I recall today as vividly as I recall that drawer full of tiny white pills—was the feeling of mistrust.

It would be a few years before I realized the full impact of what occurred that day, but in that moment I knew that I wanted to become a doctor. My Nanny trusted a four-year-child with her secret, but she did not trust her healthcare providers. I knew that I wanted to be in the position to help people like Nanny—and I understood that position would require communication, medical expertise, empathy, and above all, a foundation of trust.

Later that afternoon, my mother picked me up. Walking to the parking lot with our hands clasped, I said, "Mum, I am going to be a doctor when I grow up."

My mother smiled, but she didn't seem to think much about it at the time. Her mother, my Nanny, passed away within the year, from complications of high blood pressure. At her funeral, I remembered thinking, *Why didn't they tell her what her medications were supposed to do?* Forever branded into my memories was an essential lesson: where trust dies, mistrust blooms.

LESSON

Where trust dies, mistrust blooms.

If she had assurance that her healthcare providers and the medications they administered could help her, she would have lived longer and had a better quality of life. In fact, she might still be alive today, had someone taken time to explain her diagnosis, prognosis, and treatment so she could make better-informed decisions. Therefore, while I made the decision to be a doctor, I also decided I would never be *that* sort of doctor.

Decades later, my mother remembered my youthful declaration of purpose, but had no idea that single incident in Nanny's hospital room served as the motivating factor to help me persevere on the long and arduous journey in becoming a physician—or that it would be the foundational catalyst for my career as an orthopaedic surgeon.

IT'S A PRIVILEGE TO STAND OUT

I grew up in Birmingham, England (Handsworth, specifically), and shortly after Nanny passed, my parents moved us to the United States. Once there, we found new opportunities—and new obstacles to overcome.

Being the only girl in the classroom from England—further complicated by being Black, having a Jamaican background, and speaking with a British accent—made me different from the other kids. It was the first major roadblock I had to overcome in my new life...how to succeed when you're the only one like you in the room, with no allies, mentors, or sponsors. In tackling this first roadblock, I began assembling the psychological tools I would need and use throughout my entire life.

Along the way, I've acclimated to people second-guessing me, the same way they did my parents and my grandparents. I've become accustomed to being told *no*, but such negativity and denials have only ever fueled my fire. Spoiler alert: I can tell you from experience that it does not matter who tells you *no* or how many times they say it, so long as you don't say it to yourself.

When you're the only person who looks like you in your chosen field, there's a certain amount of pressure on you at all times. Adapting to that pressure can mean a refocus: looking at your position as a place of privilege and purpose rather than as punishment for your achievements.

I've been fortunate enough to stand on the shoulders of some very strong individuals who provided me with some powerful psychological tools. I have refined these tools in my own life experiences, and now I'm intent on offering my shoulders to stand on and my toolbox to use for the next generation after me.

PRECISION INSTRUMENTS

This book is the culmination of my journey so far, and it's one of perseverance. It's not a how-to or a humble-brag, but a chronicle of how I got here. I'm still fairly young in my surgical career, but I want to share my story and my toolbox of fortitude and resilience because I hope my story may inspire others and my tools may help others to persevere. The purpose behind these lessons of perseverance is to ensure that though I may have been the first and only in many situations, I will not be the last. My name is Dr. Lattisha Latoyah Bilbrew. I am a Black woman who is currently one of less than six Black female orthopaedic surgeons practicing in the State of Georgia. I was the second Black person to finish my orthopaedic residency training; the first Black person to complete a Hand fellowship from my program; and the first Black female orthopaedic surgeon to make partner at my practice.

My story is not a fairy tale, and it's not yet finished. As of this writing, I am also working on launching my line of designer scrubs. Things are moving quickly, and at one point, I got scared. I mean, I'm a *doctor*; what do I really know about writing a book or designing clothes? What the hell did I think I was trying to do? I started to tell myself *no* in different ways: *Stay in your lane, Dr. Bilbrew. Stick to surgery. Stick to what you know.*

Thankfully, I have two very important people I can always count on—the ultimate secret weapons in my psychological toolbox. My parents wasted no time laying down some perspective. "Lattisha, if it doesn't scare you, it's not big enough," they said. "That's how we got you and your sister here to begin with."

Touché, Mom and Dad. (This book is for them, too, and for all the previous generations who have come before me, offering their shoulders for me to stand on.)

One of the first tools they taught me was to never let fear taint your decisions. When you do, fear becomes the boulder blocking the path and halting progression on your journey. Instead of allowing fear to stop you, let your inner strength be the lever and fulcrum that moves those boulders of fear, clearing the path for success.

Nothing worth having in life is easy, and the higher you reach when pursuing your goals, the more difficult the climb will be. But you need to persevere—yes, *you*—because you have to inspire others around you to do better. When it comes to your goals and your plans for the future, you have to take the initiative to make them a reality.

To my parents' point: If you're scared, then do it afraid. *But by all means, do it.*

Even if you think you already have a mental blueprint for dealing with a certain situation, you'll still have to fine-tune and adapt in the moment. How you adjust yourself and hone your tools will make all the difference, and you'll find yourself evolving, too.

In surgery, we often describe an unskilled or obtuse surgeon by quoting Abraham Maslow: "If the only tool you have is a hammer, it is tempting to treat everything as if it were a nail." This is known as the Law of the Hammer or Law of the Instrument. It is a description of cognitive bias that occurs with overreliance on a familiar tool. It is an illustration of what happens when you have no skill set, no tools, or no instruments to help you adapt in an environment of uncertainty. When I'm performing a surgery, I have to carefully choose my instruments. Similarly, the mental instruments covered in this book will evolve over time for you as well. Choose them just as carefully.

Your own context of life experiences will fine-tune those tools, add to them, and wisely select which ones you need at any given moment. It's not enough to simply overcome life's challenges—it's *how* you overcome them that will become the measure of your character and the definition of your style. Can I physically pull you up on your journey? No. The strength to do that is already inside you. I'm simply here to encourage you and help you gain the momentum to cross the finish line with your head held high. This is not a self-help book; this book is a mirror to reflect what you are already capable of.

My shoulders are strong and supportive, and my hands are here to give you a boost. Are you ready to climb?

THE WINDRUSH WAY

After World War II, Great Britain was facing severe labor shortages, so the government actively encouraged citizens of Caribbean islands that were part of the Commonwealth (Jamaica, Trinidad, Tobago, and others) to move to England.

This initiative kickstarted a steady flow of Caribbean immigration to England from 1948 to 1970, and they became known as the Windrush generation—named for the ship that carried the first of these immigrants across the Atlantic to their new home. My maternal and paternal grandparents were among the half-million people who made this journey.

It was typical for married couples, or simply the men, to go to England and get established, then send for their families. My grandparents were no exception; it took time to earn enough money for tickets to bring the children over, so families were separated.

My mother's parents left two boys, my uncles who at that time were only a few years old, behind in Jamaica. After they immigrated to England, they had two girls, my mom and my aunt, while they were working to buy my uncles' passage. By the time they were able to send for the boys, they were already teenagers. When my father's parents came to England, they had to leave behind five children in Jamaica to be raised by relatives. It was decades before they were able to travel back to the island to see them again.

They were all extremely poor, but it meant something to be able to even get passage on the ship. These were the sacrifices my grandparents made to try to find a better life. They succeeded—and from them, I learned when you're thrust into a situation that isn't what you expected or what you asked for, the best thing you can do is stand out instead of shrink back.

LESSON:

Your sacrifice is a seed that, in the right environment, can and will grow exponentially.

DISTINGUISH YOURSELF

When my maternal grandfather came to England, he had almost nothing to his name. He was extremely intelligent, but as an elder son, he'd spent most of his life working to support the rest of his family. As a result, he probably only had a third-grade education. He left behind his parents, siblings, wife, and children, with just one small suitcase and the name of a man he'd never met, "Mr. Smith," scrawled on a piece of paper—this was to be his contact once he landed.

This wasn't much, but one suitcase and a piece of paper would be the initial instruments he needed to successfully tackle the biggest challenge of his life.

My grandfather was a tall man—he always stood head and shoulders above everyone else, so he was distinctive even in a crowd. Because of his height, he was always aware of how he looked. He dressed as well as his circumstances would allow, and he carried himself with pride: shoulders back, head high.

As a child, I noticed that my own parents always took care of their appearance, even though we weren't wealthy. Once, I even remarked to my mother, "Wow, when you and Dad go out in public, you're always so well-dressed." That's when I learned why.

My grandfather's philosophy was to distinguish yourself in the eyes of others by way of appearance and character. If you don't have the money to dress well, the manner in which you carry yourself can give you the appearance of distinction. This is part of how you stand out and make a mark on the world.

Upon his arrival in England, my grandfather also gained distinction by being friendly to everyone—not just the other Jamaicans and British, but also the Irish, who were often looked down upon by other cultural groups in England at that time. This kind of openness earned him good will in many places and broadened his social standing.

My grandfather was not only one of the few Jamaicans who learned how to drive but was one of the very few who earned a driver's license, which qualified him to operate commercial vehicles. He parlayed this skill into a job driving a street sweeper while most Black immigrants were toiling as unskilled, manual laborers.

Today, you might look at these accomplishments as less than impressive, but as a Black man living and working in a new country in those times, my grandfather was an outlier. He created a respectable life and was esteemed by those around him—and he earned and maintained his reputation through social capital.

Gain Social Capital

Social capital was my grandfather's term, and he defined it as the value of gaining upward movement without losing yourself in the process by strategically studying the environment/culture/people that you are around. My grandfather wasn't a social butterfly—he preferred to stay home with his family, read the paper, and listen to the red radio he kept next to his recliner—but he gained social capital through his strategic interactions with others. It is these tools of social capital and strategic interactions that set him apart and elevated his family to the next levels of success.

There's a difference between using social capital and being manipulative or fake. With the appropriate use of social capital, you never lose sight of the truth of who you are, where you came from, and what you are trying to accomplish; these tools are your anchors. In true Darwinian evolution, you must adapt to ensure your survival, but never change the core and substance of who you are.

My grandfather knew how to handle tense situations reasonably, and ensured those situations worked for him but never changed him for the worse. He was a very quiet man, but he was likable, and this was another trait he passed on to the next generation. My mom, his daughter, has always been a very likable woman and a popular teacher; everybody loves her because she is kind and easy to talk to. I saw that as I was growing up and used it as a model for myself, but we both inherited that tendency from my grandfather.

As a Black female surgeon navigating the world of medicine, I keep social capital at a premium, with these kinds of questions at the forefront:

→ *How am I presenting myself?*

→ *How am I distinguishing myself?*

→ *How am I using my social capital to advocate on my own behalf and to elevate others?*

→ *How can I strategically place myself in situations, in rooms, and around people to absorb, learn, replicate, and innovate?*

New Environment, New Challenges

My grandparents made lives for themselves in England, but there were plenty of sacrifices along the way. My paternal grandfather went from being a farmer—which was always where his heart was, with the land—to working in a steel mill. My paternal grandmother, a youthful country girl, became a hospital laundress.

They all had the foresight to know that moving to England was the right decision and they all distinguished themselves in different ways. My paternal grandmother became a dedicated union leader at the hospital, a communicator and negotiator who spoke up for herself and her coworkers to better their working conditions—my father called her the Jamaican Margaret Thatcher. My grandfather took his strength as a farmer and was able to weather the hazardous and physically draining environment of a steel mill. From their story, I learned that even in the most uncomfortable situation, you muster up your strength, you repurpose your skills, and you steadily move forward into success.

LESSON

Even when placed into environments that are foreign, repurpose your skill set and persevere.

The Patient Perseverer

My grandparents' journey from Jamaica to England foreshadowed my own parents' decision to move to the United States decades later. My mother's stories about my maternal grandparents reveal two crucial personality types: the peacemaker and the warrior. My maternal grandparents represented those two extremes, and I've found important parts of myself in the everyday work of finding balance between them.

The three-week boat trip my grandparents endured was not pleasant—the ships used to bring the immigrants were far from cruise ships. With only the barest of necessities, they saved enough money to take that voyage, hoping they would find something better once they arrived.

Instead, they landed somewhere that fell far short of their hopes and expectations, where they were considered lesser-than by most because of their heritage and the color of their skin. How do you go from the tropical beauty of Jamaica to the cold smog of England—from your homeland, where you are among the majority, to a country where you face racism every day? How do you make a successful life when the odds are stacked against you, and your family still depends on you?

My maternal grandfather, a born peacemaker, embodied what I call "the patient perseverer." He took on every challenge with an eye toward his personal priorities for his family, which is something many people find difficult to do, even today. A second income would have meant more money coming in and greater prosperity, but my grandfather wanted to make sure that my grandmother didn't have to work; this would allow her to focus her energy on their children. He worked long hours and built a reputation as a good worker, which also fed into his social capital. In order to ensure their financial stability, he saw his responsibilities to his family and his job as a privilege rather than a burden.

I relate to that on a different level—my responsibility is to my patients, and like many doctors, I'm on call at the hospital most days. I like it. This is my privilege, so I don't mind getting those 2:00 a.m. calls, even on days when I'm dead tired. It's not that I'm a glutton for punishment; I just see it as another chance to help someone who needs my skills and live up to my responsibilities. I inherited these tools from my grandfather; they are an intrinsic part of me, as they were for him.

LESSON

Shift your perspective—look at your job and your responsibilities as a privilege rather than a burden.

The Worrier-Warrior

My maternal grandmother, Nanny, was an imposing woman—when she wore heels, she was almost as tall as my grandfather. As I mentioned in the Introduction, she was headstrong. She was the kind of person other people didn't mess with, because she was never afraid to fight. In many ways, my maternal grandmother was the opposite of her husband—whereas he was the patient perseverer, she was a worrier and a warrior who never lost a battle.

My grandparents lived in a second-floor flat with no indoor plumbing, and at one point, they ran afoul of a city ordinance. In Handsworth at that time, everyone was supposed to be in charge of turning on their own streetlamps in the evening and turning them off in the morning. Police officers, called "bobbies" in England, would write citations for people who didn't turn their lamps on or off at the right time. My grandparents had already made this mistake a few times.

One night, my grandmother looked out the window and saw a bobby turn *off* their streetlamp and start to write them a ticket for it. She knew what it meant, and she got angry. My grandfather told her not to worry about it, that they would just pay the ticket. As the patient-perseverer, this seemed like the best course of action.

My grandmother was the worrier-warrior, however, so she wasn't having it. "If we do that, we may not eat next week," she told him. "Our electricity might get shut off. We don't have the money."

Then my fearless grandmother leaned out the window to shout at the bobby, "I saw what you did!" Grabbing their chamber pot, which was full, she dumped the entire pot of piss down onto the bobby's head—even as my grandfather begged her not to do it.

My mother, who was about eight years old at the time, said, "This is it. Mum's going to jail. They're going to come and bombard the house. Dad's going to get beat up."

Instead, the bobby went away without giving them the ticket. And in fact, that was the *last* time anyone in the neighborhood got written up for their streetlamps. Maybe they were afraid of her, or maybe it was the embarrassment of the situation—imagine that bobby having to go back to the station with the stench of urine and explain what had happened—but being a warrior, she got the job done. Not just for her family, but for her entire community.

But my grandmother was also a worrier—that's why I call her a "worrier-warrior." When it came to my grandfather, she was his anchor and his focus; she was the reason he could be so patient and persevering, the reason he could manage all the changes and the struggles he faced in England. She also worried about him, however, and about their family, both those in England and those in Jamaica. She always fought her own battles, but she worried about how being radical could also affect her family.

This tendency to worry alongside that tendency to be in battle mode contributed to her health problems later in life. She was living in a society and in a situation that didn't give her room to rest, and it wore her down psychologically and physically.

LESSON

You can't continually function at 100 miles per hour and expect to keep running smoothly.

This is the part of my grandmother I remember the most; it is the reason I focus on balance and making sure I don't fall on either extreme of the spectrum of worrier-warrior. I'm not going to throw a pot of piss at a cop, but I'm also not going to worry myself to death. I focus on keeping myself at a good balance, although that's easier said than done.

Sometimes when you're in a situation where something is blatantly unjust, you have to step forward. You have to be the radical person who says, "I'm going to be the light here. I may go to jail, but I'm going to be the last person who goes to jail for something they shouldn't have to go to jail for."

Admittedly, that part of me is not always intrinsic. Leaning on my tendency to be peaceful, I have to deliberately dig deeper to channel my inner warrior. When I'm feeling passive or indecisive, that is when it's time to let people know I won't be taking their crap. I call upon my grandmother's strength and carefully weigh my choices and course of action in the process.

LESSON

Life is a balance. Find your steady in-between.

YOU, ME, AND THE STEADY IN-BETWEEN

As you establish yourself in life, your social capital grows comparable to the amount of time and energy invested in its development. My paternal grandfather, the farmer-turned-steel worker, always told my father his hope was in education, because it was the key to freedom. Education was essentially the fuel that powered the machine that is Social Capital. His generation worked with their hands as their way of planting the seeds for their children to have a better life. "If you plant nothing, you gain nothing," he would say.

So what are you planting? Is it a seed that will help to improve your status in life, or that could help the next generation improve? How are you building and using your social capital to the fullest?

While bearing this in mind, I also strive to remember to balance my inner peacemaker with my inner warrior. We have to know when we need to be the peacemaker and when we need to be the warrior—and we need to have the wisdom to determine which is appropriate for any given situation.

Even my grandfather realized this truth. My grandmother's fire must have been part of what attracted him to her in the first place and made him think, "I'm going to marry that one." He knew he was more passive and patient, and knew he could suffer and survive, but he also knew no one could be like that *all* the time.

He was right. Even if your dominant personality is to be the peacemaker, sometimes you have to be radical. Sometimes, the patient perseverer tool is not going to help—that's when it's time to turn on the warrior mode. You have to get in tune with that part of you because you have to be able to access it when you need it.

Find your balance—your steady in-between—because that's when you will be most effective; you can make waves and distinguish yourself, even if (*especially* if) you are in a situation you weren't expecting, or one that has the deck stacked against you.

Remember: in order to stand out, there will be times you must stand up, stand down, or sit quietly. Choose your battles and your weapons carefully in order to distinguish yourself in the most effective way possible. That way, you'll be in a position to do something else even *more* important: create a vision *and* a foundation for the next generation. My grandparents set that vision and foundation for my parents, and they—like my grandfather—saw it as their duty and privilege to do the same for my sister and me.

To view pictures of Dr. Bilbrew's grandfather, grandmother, and the rest of her family, visit www.drlattishabilbrew.com.

2

THE NEXT GENERATION

The term "glass ceiling" is frequently used when it comes to the limits society puts on certain groups of people in terms of success and upward mobility. The idea is that those who are stopped by the glass ceiling—namely, women and minorities—can still see the opportunities above them. They just can't access them.

Most people in these groups already know there's going to be a ceiling somewhere in every endeavor. They (we) have been trained to expect it all their lives, and often, they've been subjected to accept the limitation every glass ceiling implies: *you can go this far, but no further.*

Meanwhile, those who aren't affected by that barrier can pretend there's no ceiling at all.

There are a multitude of problems with accepting the concept of a glass ceiling. The most stagnating is that if you can already see it, you will surely hit it. When that happens, we become so focused on the ceiling itself that we forget we can get past it, if we are determined enough.

My parents saw the glass ceiling in their lives in England, and they became determined to leave in order to keep it from trapping their daughters. They had heard about my grandparents' journeys from Jamaica their whole lives, so they knew it was possible to start over and to find broader horizons in a new country. For them, that country was the United States. Their choice to immigrate there would change the trajectory of my life.

LESSON

Glass ceilings are meant to be broken.

THE ENTHUSIASTIC ADVENTURER

If you've ever had a friend or family member who was always up for anything, then you have some idea of what my father is like.

Though he has a playful disposition, Dad has never been afraid of moving forward. He loves trying new things—the more uncommon, the better—which satisfies his playfulness and his drive. That energy and sense of adventure drove my parents' decision to leave England for America, and it's been one of the hallmarks of his entire life.

My father grew up as one of ten siblings, so he got used to standing out in a crowd at an early age. After secondary school, he went to art school for graphic design. In 1979, he moved to Saudi Arabia to be a graphic artist. He was only nineteen, and this journey made him the first person in his family to board a plane.

Much like my maternal grandfather, my father had already found an anchor in the woman he loved. He returned to England and proposed to my mother when he returned.

Since he wasn't the only one with a sense of adventure, she accepted.

THE PASSIONATE PLANNER

Since the age of fourteen, my mother knew her true future wasn't in Great Britain. "I always knew I was going to live in America one day," she said. "I just always felt it was a better place." It was the kind of thing people might deem a childhood fantasy, especially for a little Black girl in England, the daughter of immigrants herself, but she held onto that conviction and nurtured it until it became a reality.

Like my father, my mother started out as an artist, earning her first degree in textiles and art. However, between the two of them, she was the scholar and the planner. I didn't learn until much later in life that she also had dreams of being a doctor, although they were thwarted by people telling her *no*, much the same way people tried with me. However, she had a talent for training others, so education became her passion in life, both personally and professionally.

Once my parents were married and settled down, they started their family, but they were always mindful of the *greater-than* element of their future. Even the most enthusiastic adventurer needs a co-pilot who knows how to plan and strategize accordingly—otherwise, they'd get lost along the way. Luckily for my father, he found the perfect partner in my mother, who not only carved out the path for them to immigrate successfully to America, but who was the first to dream that dream for us all.

The catalyst that truly set things into motion came when she was up for the headmistress position at her school. She was the most qualified applicant for the job, but was passed over in lieu of someone with inferior qualifications...and who was

White. It was a textbook glass-ceiling experience: *this far—but no further.*

BECOMING *GREATER-THAN*

My mother and father appreciated the struggles their parents endured to establish their lives in England, and they knew those struggles had all been taken on in the name of giving them and their siblings better lives. There was a certain amount of pressure on them in that regard. It would be a slap in the face if my parents, who benefitted from a full education, accomplished less than their parents, who had had only basic schooling but were fueled by aspirations revolutionary for their time.

My parents understood they had to be *greater-than* in order to not only be successful but also honor their parents who came before them. The preceding generation sets the foundation in place and provides the building blocks for the next generation to succeed; everything my grandparents did with their lives provided the substructure that my parents could build upon to shape their futures.

The ability to get an education was an important part of that future, because it provided training for more specialized and rewarding jobs. Remember, "If you plant nothing, you gain nothing," as my father's father said. But it was also about hitting important milestones and ensuring that each generation maintained that forward-thinking vision that provided a secure foundation for the next.

During their first decade or so of marriage, my parents had already achieved so much that they could have looked at their lives as having fulfilled that *greater-than* promise. However, when my mother felt she could no longer trust in her upward mobility in England, she worried about her daughters' futures as well.

A Plan Comes Together

In the mid-1990s, my parents, my sister, and I were fully established in our Handsworth community, with family, friends, and church to anchor us. My sister and I walked to school every day. My father ran a successful business with multiple corporate contracts, including one for the city of Birmingham, and my mother was a teacher on the verge of becoming a school headmistress. When I look back and think about it, we traveled quite a bit—we took trips to Jamaica to visit family, Spain for Christmas, and Disney World multiple times in the year.

I didn't fully realize it at the time, but between our social standing and our financial stability, we were very well-off for a family of four from Birmingham. My parents worked very hard to create that life for us.

And then…we left it all behind.

LESSON

Never get too comfortable; it is in a place of discomfort that we grow the most.

Even now, I can't quite get over the audacity of my parents choosing to move to the United States in 1995. That would be a huge life change even now, when you can easily Google, *How do I immigrate?* and get detailed checklists of what you need to do. My parents conducted their research independently and together, in addition to working and raising children. It took them years to map out the entire plan and save up the money to make it all work; however, despite their differences in perspective—or perhaps because of them—my parents were a near-perfect duo to accomplish this otherwise monumental goal.

During those years of planning, my mother searched for teaching jobs in America—because, of course, we weren't going to move without having already established employment. No slip of paper with "Mr. Smith" written on it for this journey—my parents had to establish their own employment in advance.

I learned years later that those Florida vacations were actually part of their planning process. My mother used those trips to interview for teaching positions.

During one of those trips, she clicked with one school so well—using that social capital that my grandfather taught her—that she convinced them to not only hire her, but hold the position for her until she could complete the immigration process. It took another year and a half, but that job was waiting for her when we moved to Florida.

How does anyone make something like that happen? My mother understood the first step in winning is not just believing, but *knowing* you are qualified and deserve to be there. She is confident in talking to people, but more importantly, she is confident in herself—because she knows she has the education and the skills to back it up. Her social capital is solid, and when it's combined with her likable personality, she's the kind of person other people want to have around them.

Visually, I will always remember my mother interviewing in a red suit, head held high. It is the reason even today Red is my power color. When I need to feel empowered, I wear Red. When I operate in surgery, I still channel that confidence and feeling of "I belong," and thus, my surgical loupes…are Red.

LESSON

Confidence requires qualifications, but also the embodiment of a feeling you can adorn at will—much like accessorizing a well-tailored suit.

Decades later, my mother admitted that had she gotten that headmistress position, we probably wouldn't have left England. "I would have felt like I was moving up," she explained. "But when they gave it to someone less qualified than me, that was enough for me to say, 'It's time to go.'" Ultimately, she wasn't going to raise her daughters where they were always in danger of being stripped of the relatively few opportunities available to them.

Once my mother's job was lined up, my parents accelerated their plans, and suddenly our whole household was changing in preparation for the move. My father was selling off things in the house, even selling his car. While we were always quiet about our plans, things were obviously changing, and our neighbors took notice.

People were whispering about us and wondering what we were up to. My parents were hyperaware that they were not supportive of our plans, so we were told to keep quiet.

LESSON

Build in silence.

"When you build something," they would explain, "sometimes, you have to build it quietly, because the majority might not approve." This idea of "building in silence" kept their plans close to their hearts instead of putting them on display, where they might get derailed.

As a result, we did not discuss our Florida vacations with anyone else. Instead, we built in silence.

On the day we left England, only three or four people knew about our departure. We sold everything, packed one suitcase per person, and took off in the middle of the night. There was no Facebook or Instagram "big news!" post, or even an old-fashioned, handwritten note. They woke up, and we were gone.

Coming to America

No matter how quietly you build, however, you are always going to make noise when you embark on something so big. I have learned that when someone starts to make noise in their life, other people get startled. If you're working toward a dream they don't understand—if your dream is big enough or different enough—people who aren't truly supportive of you can get scared. And because they don't understand that kind of fear, it can make people intimidated and resentful. My parents knew that, so we never talked openly about our plans, even to our closest friends. My parents had certain hopes for their life in the U.S., both for themselves and for their two daughters, and their community did not understand or support their strategic planning and ideology for the next generation.

Historically, racism was more of an issue in America than in England, especially in the South, which was where we would be living. The irony was that there was still much more opportunity in America for education and employment, so—at least for my parents—the move was worth the risk, culture shock and all. We were giving up a little to gain a lot.

LESSON

There will always be doubts and doubters. Never fear what you may lose; be inspired by what you may gain, and confidently move forward.

America may have been the lesser of two evils, but my parents knew that by immigrating, they were giving their children—the next generation—*their* best foundation to succeed. The value in this choice was immeasurable, and I've never stopped being grateful for my parents' strength of mind. I love thinking of them in terms of the adventurer and the planner, working together to achieve a goal most people even today would consider a pipe dream. My parents always say they were "on the same sheet of music" during this time of their marriage; that mentality allowed them to not just conceptualize the plan to immigrate, but to strategize and actually execute it.

I was seven years old when we moved, and as far as I was concerned, I was moving to Disney World, so even though I would be leaving behind my Christmas toys and my friends, I was excited about this new adventure. It didn't matter that we started out small in Florida; we lived in an apartment, our furniture was sparse and cheap, and our toys were from the dollar store. My child's mind saw it as going on a permanent vacation. With my mother's dreams and plans guiding the way, and my father's energy and enthusiasm propelling them both forward, we arrived.

THE ADVENTURE CONTINUES

It's been nearly three decades since my family's move to Florida, and we've had our share of ups and downs during that time. My parents worked side-by-side to bring our young family across the Atlantic. In time, they would divorce, but they remain friends to this day.

I have asked my parents, the adventurer and the planner, "Would you do it all again?"

Without hesitation, the answer is always one word: "Absolutely." For them, it boils down to never settling for what is in front of you if you can envision doing something greater.

My mother always taught me not to be afraid of the decisions I make. Even if you agonize over them, once they are made, you have to be confident in those decisions, even if they aren't popular ones. She's always felt following her gut instinct and trusting what was inside her was what led her to being brave enough to move forward—especially when it came to following a dream some may have felt was immature or foolish. If you focus on something, you can materialize it—but you have to have the conviction and the confidence to build the dream into a strategy and take it all the way to execution, even if it takes years.

LESSON

Accomplishing a dream requires a strategic plan and, ultimately, execution of that plan.

This is the way my mother feels about our journey to America, and how she and my father worked together to make it a reality. Even today, my mother would tell me, "Don't be afraid to make mistakes," while my father poignantly would add, "There are no mistakes—only adjustments."

These days, my father has fully embraced being a grandfather, having become my son's full-time nanny—and I'm so thankful for that. "The vision has to have excitement," he says. "Because it's the excitement that drives you to move forward, despite the potential risks. If you spend all your time on the path just looking at every potential negative, you're going to get discouraged, but if you can keep true to the excitement of the initial vision, you'll keep the fire burning, and that fire is your fuel." He is one of the most successful people in his family, and I attribute that to his energy and attitude when it comes to embracing new endeavors.

Whether he is embracing his role as an entrepreneur or a nanny, he brings his sense of adventure to everyday activities, making games out of everything from mealtimes to taking out the trash. With his never-ending source of energy, adventure, and creativity, I have asked him what can be done if you don't have that adventurous spirit. What if you don't feel brave enough?

"Ask yourself what's important," he said. "Are you content with where you are? Are you happy?" If the answer is *no*, then you have to find that vision of what will make you happy—because whatever it is that makes you truly happy will also make you brave. "If you're not happy with who you are becoming, then it's time to start figuring out what you can do to change it."

Amen, Dad.

BREAKING FREE

When I look at my own life and my sister's life, I can see the results of my parents' decision to immigrate. Not only do I admire my parents for their fortitude, but I am also aware that we owe them so much. As far as I'm concerned, they moved us out from under a major part of that glass ceiling. Therefore, it would be up to us to leverage that advantage and reach for the limitless sky.

This is not to say I never came up against a glass ceiling during my education and in my chosen profession—but it does mean that, thanks to them, I was better equipped to break through. Thanks to them, I recognized the glass ceiling as something thin and fragile, a feeble social barrier based on prejudice and declarations of *no* from others.

LESSON

Stand firmly on the shoulders of those who came before you, because they are giving you greater vision and clarity to see the fragility of a glass ceiling.

Today, I look at my son and think about what I can do to help him the same way. I think about how I need to challenge myself, and push myself to achieve more—to elevate my own version of "greater," and honor the generation that came before me. And to build a better foundation for the next.

I also think about how my decisions and my actions affect others. Social capital isn't about elevating just yourself; it means you can elevate those around you, and sometimes you can do that as a living example, as a trailblazer. Trailblazing alerts others to a new path or a new opportunity. In each scenario, the trailblazer and the follower exercise humility by recognizing the value of starting over.

Back in Handsworth, many thought we were crazy for moving to the U.S. to start afresh. The truly crazy thing? Over the next ten years or so, four or five families from our community immigrated to the U.S., just like us. Those families took a chance on a risky adventure they might never have even dreamed of if my parents hadn't done it first.

Sometimes, a little empowerment is all it takes to help you realize it might be worth taking a step back, especially if it means building enough momentum to catapult you five steps forward. That's a mindset I've embraced my whole life, through thick and thin, and I have never regretted it.

Along the way, you have to find your own foundation of support, whether family or friends, personal or professional—but never forget, the trail you blaze is your own.

LESSON

Just as you should never limit yourself, you must never settle for the limits others put on you. Glass is fragile...and it can be broken.

3

THE NEW GIRL

I've always loved a challenge. Even as a very young child, I had a tendency to step up and take on any challenge that came my way, regardless of my realistic capabilities. If I wasn't reined in by my parents or caregivers, I never shied away, even when I definitely should have.

Case in point: One of the most important lessons of my early childhood was rooted in self-awareness and the importance of knowing my own limits. It involves singing in church...but not in a good way.

At my church in Handsworth, we had a huge convention every year that brought in thousands of people. When I was about five years old, my best friend Zoe was invited to sing on the stage in front of everyone at the convention. Zoe was a beautiful singer, and everybody clapped and praised her.

And because Zoe was my best friend and she could sing, I thought *I* could sing, too. I thought there was no reason I shouldn't be allowed to get up there on stage—despite the fact that my parents knew damn well that I could not sing, and tried their best to stop me. I insisted, however, to the point that they just let it happen.

Bear in mind: this was a Jamaican-British church, and it was not a regular service, but a national convention. The people who attended came to be entertained during praise and worship. If you got up in front of them, they were expecting something good.

So I got up there, and I belted out, "This Little Light of Mine."

When I finished, nobody clapped. Nothing but crickets in that audience. Tough crowd! Bless my parents, though. When I ran off the stage crying, they were there, ready to love on me and make me feel better.

This was one of my earliest lessons in self-awareness—knowing my own limits in a practical way—and I'm grateful that my parents were realistic with me about my goals while also being supportive of my endeavors. In fact, I learned a few hard lessons that day, though of course they wouldn't sink in fully until much later.

First, it's important to listen to people wiser than you. You have to have someone guiding you through the process, someone you trust.

Second, I needed that little moment as a five-year-old to realize what my limitations are. I remember when the first "American Idol" debuted, and I was flabbergasted to see so many adults do what amounted to my five-year-old self's performance on that convention stage—only their performance was broadcasted in front of millions of television viewers.

I can't help but wonder where *their* support system went wrong. Where did their internal self-analysis go haywire?

That day at the convention, my parents tried to stop me—and as a parent myself now, I absolutely understand why—but in the end, they understood how confident I was in myself and consequently knew I had to learn this lesson the hard way. Little-girl Lattisha saw the challenge and wanted to jump in headfirst.

LESSON

Be confident, but also be prepared...
and most importantly, be qualified.

You can have all the ambition in the world and tackle every challenge head-on, but without self-awareness, it's going to be that much more difficult to succeed. Self-awareness is strength; it allows you to strategize and prioritize, taking your plans to the next level.

I bless my parents for knowing that truth, and helping me find my way to it. They were never dream-killers, but they knew I would always need a dose of reality as I navigated my childhood after we moved to America.

As it turned out, being a Black British girl in a Florida school wasn't exactly a comfortable role to inhabit, especially when we first arrived.

LEARNING CURVE

Going into an American school from the British school system while speaking like someone caught between a British and Jamaican accent led to various challenges for my sister and me—some my family anticipated, and others we didn't.

In addition to not yet fully understanding the academic metrics for Florida schools, we already had a strike against us: we weren't the typical age for our grade level in America. English schools start earlier, so we were a year younger than the other kids in our respective grade levels. They wanted to bump us down a grade; never mind that we could demonstrate the skills and knowledge to prove we were ready for our respective grades. My mother had to speak to the superintendent so we could enter school at the proper grade level and not be held back.

Once we got past that, we got hit with the ESL assignment, which would have put us in classrooms with primarily Spanish-speaking students.

The obvious issue? We spoke English. As a first language.

We had no trouble comprehending the material; our accents and our British spellings were what got us slated for ESL classes. My mother knew what was happening: two little Black girls were entering the school, and they were intelligent and would be the youngest in their classes. But we had thick accents and spelled *flavor* with an added *u*, so obviously we needed to be placed in classes geared toward non-English speakers (sarcasm). They were setting us up for failure.

LESSON

Don't be surprised when those who are expected to propel you forward strategize to set you back.

Can you imagine how our education would have been affected by this? If we'd just gone along with it, our academic potential and progress would have stalled out before it had a chance to begin. My sister and I were too young to stand up for ourselves back then, but we have a stalwart, savvy advocate in our mother.

She saw through this right away—and how could she not? I mean, if we had been two little White girls with British accents, we'd have been fawned over at our new school. Of that, I have no doubt. She always told us that if anything was intent on holding us back or prolonging our journey to success, we wouldn't be participating. Not her kids. Not ever.

Once again, she fought for her daughters to receive fair treatment—and won. My grandmother would have been proud of her fierceness.

There are always going to be people who doubt your ability to persevere and succeed, and they are going to try to underestimate you and pass you over despite your qualifications and your demonstrated abilities. In those times, especially if you have no advocate for support, you have to know yourself and your capabilities so you can stand up for yourself.

When you're different—when you're the minority—you're generally at a disadvantage in the eyes of others. "Different" is considered a weakness by those who doubt you, but it is your difference that makes you powerful.

> **LESSON**
>
> **There is power in being the only one like you in the room, because that's where you can affect change.**

FINDING MY OWN VOICE

When you're in a new situation, you don't know what you don't know, so your first priority has to be learning the metrics for success. Once eight-year-old me settled into my classes, I learned by trial and error, with a healthy dose of dedicated work. My mother and father provided a great support system at home, but during the school day, I had to be my own advocate. So I got busy.

My first hurdle was the American grading system, which I discovered was different from the British system, when another student made fun of me for receiving a *B* while he received an *A*. I studied harder, and the next time, I got an *A* too. After getting marked down for using British spellings and terms, I worked harder to learn the American spellings of common words. Before long, I was consistently making straight *A*s.

Another, more systemic obstacle proved more difficult to overcome—and it's one I still struggle with not only as an immigrant, but as a Black person in America: the subject of Black history. Let me tell you, learning Black history in American schools was a shock to my system, after having studied it across the diaspora in England. So many times, I was told I was incorrect when I contradicted something I was taught from the school history book, so I would go research it independently. More often than not, I'd find out I was right—but I still failed to change my teachers' minds, or get them to change the way they taught this historical material.

Their denial frustrated me, but even so, it proved to be a good experience for me in the long run. This became my first real experience with actively seeking out the truth rather than accepting what I was told. I never stopped challenging what I was taught, and acquiring truth and knowledge became more essential than proving I was right in class.

All this focus on knowledge and academic excellence didn't make me popular, but it was me being my authentic self—and that's exactly who I wanted and needed to be. I got teased for being a nerd, but what made me the biggest target was my accent. I was a Black girl with a thick British accent in the South.

My internal monologue probably went something like this: *You don't like that I sound different than everyone else? You think that makes me weak? Fine. I'm going to take the opportunity to really speak.*

So when I saw the school sponsored an oratory contest, I saw my chance. Challenge accepted.

The contest was the red flag and I was the bull—I charged right into it. Then I surprised everyone, including myself, by winning and making it to the regional competition.

At that point, my father stepped in to help coach me, and from him I learned tricks to maximize my impact when speaking to crowds, lessons I still utilize today. He taught me how to lower my tone of voice, which was important, because mine was high and squeaky. He also taught me how to time my breathing when speaking, and to emphasize certain words to affect intonation.

Yes, I won the regional competition, but I gained so much more than an award. To this day, any time I speak in public, I always flash back to that time of vulnerability in my life. My drive to become a strong speaker stems directly from the challenge of taking something others saw as a weakness and turning it into a weapon.

LESSON

Any perceived negative can become something that defines you in a positive way and improves your self-awareness.

NO ONE PLAYS THE OBOE

Another challenge I accepted was joining the school band. I was in sixth grade.

The band director, Dr. Bob Condor, went through all the instruments. He was a trombonist himself, so he started with the brass, and then he went through the woodwinds. When I picked up an oboe, he gave me a look. Taking the oboe from me, he showed me how to play a few notes. At the time, I didn't think much of it, but as an adult, I know he only played for a few seconds because he didn't know how to play it very well.

"No one chooses this one, it's too difficult to master," he said, handing it back to me.

I could see why: that particular oboe was nothing fancy, and it was... well, we're talking a certain amount of disgusting. It looked horrible, and it had sounded fairly horrible when he played it. My expression must have communicated some of these thoughts, because Dr. Bob spoke like he was replying to me when he said, “This is one of the hardest instruments to play.”

My fate was sealed.

Red flag + bull = you know where this is going with Lattisha.

“That’s the one I want,” I insisted.

We always have choices on the paths we take, and there are all kinds of reasons to take the easy route. That’s also where you’re going to distinguish yourself in the eyes of others and build your reputation.

LESSON

Sometimes you have to choose the hardest road, because that’s where you’re going to learn the most—especially about yourself.

I could have chosen another instrument and mastered it. A dozen other girls wanted to play the flute because it was cute, and we could have all become friends playing the flute together—but I never would have stood out.

Instead, I chose the oboe, and I worked my ass off to learn to play it, with the help of Dr. Bob, who's now my friend via social media. From then on, I became known in the band world as the little Black girl who played the oboe.

And like all things strategic involving growth and social capital, it carried the potential of uplifting others. Dr. Bob wasn't wrong; very few people choose the oboe, and because it's a rare sight in school bands, kids don't always think of it as an option. Then stubborn me comes along and refuses to be told *no*, and suddenly people recognize it can be done. I truly hope I functioned as a trailblazer in that regard and not only influenced others to be more open to that instrument but also normalized Black girls in orchestra. I hope I was an echo of my parents influencing others to immigrate.

Most importantly, taking on the challenge kept me from being complacent and settling for the easy road. Had I failed at playing the oboe, the experience still would have been a fulfilling one in that sense: I pushed myself out of my comfort zone and gained a new self-awareness along the way.

COMPLACENCY IS THE REAL DREAM-KILLER

As we progress through life, we discover that certain things are intrinsic to us—things that come naturally, without being taught, regardless of our age or situation. When you find what is intrinsic to you, embrace it and use it to build your goals. For me personally, they serve as the cornerstones of who I am today.

For example, I have a strong desire to help others and a sense of creativity. I've built one of those into a surgical practice of which I am extremely proud, and I'm hoping to build the other into a new endeavor as a fashion designer. Yes, those two things don't seem like they should coexist in one person; it doesn't matter if they *should*, because they *do*.

I have identified what's intrinsic to me by walking through all the challenges, successes, and failures along the way, and from the support system that helped guide me through them until I could find my own way. Without rising to all these challenges, I couldn't have earned the self-awareness I need to know myself and to be confident in my capabilities—to make my journey a fulfilling one, even as it continues.

Make no mistake: I may have achieved many of my goals, but I'm still on my journey. As long as you're alive, you're on the journey, and if something isn't challenging you along the way, you risk falling into complacency.

And complacency, not failure, is the real dream-killer. Failures (or, as my father states, *adjustments*) are crucial to our learning process and building self-awareness, and though they may sometimes be unpleasant, they're part of how we grow.

4

FAILING UPWARD

Once upon a very brief time, there was a pre-teen named Lattisha who thought for a second she might make her name not in the medical field, but in the world of basketball.

My sister and I were healthy, athletic kids—we played tennis with our father for fun, and ran on treadmills after school every day. Meanwhile, I was already making excellent grades and playing first-chair oboe. In searching out more challenges to add to my accomplishments, it was natural that, like many kids, I would set my sights on becoming an athlete of some kind. When I found out people were trying out for the basketball team, I figured I should too. Why not? Just like anything else, if I tried to do it, I'd be great at it, right?

I went to the tryouts, and to put it gently, your girl was not a natural. I could run and I could dribble—but both at the same time, plus aiming and shooting the ball on the fly? It felt like a monumental task, even as I watched the other girls around me demonstrating those skills with little apparent effort. *What the hell?* I thought, astounded and already beginning to wear out. *I should be able to do this!*

Although my confidence was already beginning to dwindle, I applied everything I had to the challenge, with my father's voice on repeat in my head: Play through the pain, Lattisha.

I ran, dribbled, and shot that basketball all day, but it just didn't go through the hoop. So the next day, I checked the team roster, and my name wasn't on the list. But at the very bottom of the page, there was my name and next to it, in parentheses: (Team Manager). In my mind, I made the team!

When I told my family that night that I'd made the team, my father was thrilled. "Way to go!" he said, grinning. He loved basketball. "What position are you playing?"

Uh-oh. "Manager," I said, making sure to keep my smile bright.

His smile, however, lost some wattage. "Okay," he said. "Congratulations, Lattisha."

Despite his skepticism, I still wanted to show him I could do this—the manager was still part of the team. I'd gotten something from that tryout, and I wasn't going to let it go so easily.

At my first practice, I showed up early, ready to go. I spent most of that time delivering water to the players—and while that was somewhat disappointing, I still felt honor-bound to my position. It could potentially lead to more, I reasoned; if it helped me become better at basketball, I might be able to actually play during the season. At the very least, it would be something for my college applications.

My parents, however, weren't so optimistic. After that first practice, they sat me down for a heavy dose of reality. "Lattisha, we're not going to be continuing with basketball," they said.

I argued a little at first, but it didn't take long for me to see their point. While a role as team manager had some worth, it wasn't going to add anything significant to my success later on. Most importantly, I. Was. Not. Good. At. Basketball!

"Take a hard look at your future," my father advised. "Are you going to be a basketball player, or a doctor?"

Now I felt a little ashamed. "A doctor," I admitted.

Unless I devoted a significant amount of time to practicing basketball—to the possible detriment of my academic focus—I probably wasn't ever going to be good enough to even be on the actual team. And let's face it: even if I made the high-school team, the NBA was never going to be a part of my future, because any talent I might cultivate wasn't going to turn out to be exceptional enough. My energy would be more productive focused elsewhere.

I talked to the coach the very next day and quit my job as team manager. And even though I felt like I let myself and the team down, my parents encouraged me to think about it differently. "There are no failures," my father said. "Just adjustments. You're recalculating."

My father, being a bit more blunt, went on to say, "Don't be afraid to make honest mistakes. But don't dwell on them, either. Know your strengths in life and recognize your weaknesses."

HOOP DREAMS, READJUSTED

When it came to my hoop dreams, the reality was clear: I just wasn't good at basketball. It was the first experience I had at failing to do something I had hoped to do well. My best wasn't good enough and I didn't have much choice but to accept it and move on. This experience taught me the value of adjustment and realistic expectations. Since that time, I've gotten comfortable admitting if I'm not proficient at something, especially when it's not crucial to my priorities and progression toward my goals. On the road to becoming a surgeon—getting stellar grades in math? Necessary. Playing basketball as the team manager? Not so much.

LESSON

Recognize and categorize your strengths and weaknesses as early into your journey as possible.

And you know what? I was okay with that. If you enjoy basketball or any extra-curricular activity, by all means enjoy and participate. If something or someone is pulling you away from your upward progression, however, consider reevaluating its purpose on your journey. Most importantly, never be ashamed or embarrassed if you have to make that adjustment.

I'm thankful my parents were supportive of me trying out, and for giving me a chance to try to manage the team, but I'm even more thankful they sat me down for a reality check. And I'm thankful that the termination of my hoop dreams provided my first real opportunity to experience and learn how to accept failure. In the words of a wise friend, even the opportunity to experience failure and readjust into greatness is a privilege.

HARDWARE FAILURE

Failure can be defined as the lack of success, but if you consider it more as success turned inside out, failure still provides an opportunity to prevail. You learn from failure as you do from success, just from another angle—and with a little more pain involved.

Basketball was a failure, because it was beyond my capabilities in a fundamental way. I knew so little about the game and so little about how to play it that my inability to perform should have come as no surprise. Had I prepared a little more before the tryouts, I might have improved enough to make the team; however, I also might have been discouraged from even attempting to try out.

I still look back on my brief career in basketball as a positive in other ways, however. Even though I may not have made the team, I was picked to be the manager, and that was an accomplishment too. It meant the coaches recognized my spirit of perseverance, despite my ability to do a lay-up or not (and trust me, *I could not*). Maybe it was my eagerness, maybe my energy, maybe my determination... whatever it was, they saw it, and that means something to me even today.

It's great to try things and attempt new challenges. It's also great to take a step back and reassess if things aren't working out. Is what you're doing *really for you*? Will it add something vital to your life?

If the answer is *no*, readjusting your choices is an option—and sometimes, it's the best and most realistic one.

When do you know your potential success has been turned inside out? How do you know when it's time to try something else? The same way you find out anything: you examine it from all angles and get advice from people you trust.

As an orthopaedic surgeon, I have to keep a sharp eye out for a phenomenon known as hardware failure. If a patient who's recently had surgery involving the use of a plate and screws begins to complain that something hurts or doesn't feel right, I have to act fast. I can determine hardware failure only after X-rays of the affected body part and a detailed clinical examination—and then I assess all elements to figure out exactly how, when, and where the hardware has failed: Is it the plate or rod? Is it one or more of the screws? Is it the way it was placed? Is it due to the patient's comorbidities or bone quality?

I can't know for certain how to help the patient until I've done a thorough assessment of what went wrong. Then, I can recalculate, readjust, and fix the problem.

So, when you're faced with failure, look inward at what you've done and then look outward at the environment. What kind of failure are we talking about here?

Failure is often grouped into one of three categories:

- → Unavoidable failure
- → Intelligent failure
- → Preventable failure

Unavoidable failures, as you might be able to surmise from the name, are the result of the complex variables within your journey. These tend to be minuscule and negligible in the grand scheme, but if you get too comfortable with them, they will recur and snowball into massive failures. I experienced these types of small failures during my transition to American schools—there were just some areas in which I wasn't prepared or knowledgeable enough to prevent certain errors. By working hard to overcome my lack of understanding and conquer my ignorance, however, I was able to never make the same mistake twice and prevent the regularity of these "unavoidable failures."

Intelligent failures arise from trial and error as you begin to test your capabilities along the way. When you try something different or push yourself in a new direction, you'll sometimes find that it won't work. I always think of my father's concept of readjustment when I think of this type of failure—if you don't succeed, recalibrate and take the wisdom of the experience with you. My brief career in basketball falls in this category.

Preventable failures are the ones you want to avoid whenever possible: the major, deliberate deviations from what you know is right or optimal. If you have to be up at 5:00 a.m. for your rounds at the hospital, staying out to party all night is the wrong decision—and you can apply this example in just about every context. If you don't take precautions, you're going to be the cause of preventable failures; while everyone makes the occasional mistake, anyone who winds up causing multiple preventable failures is going to find themselves defined by them.

Remember: an abundance of small failures can sometimes be an indication of self-sabotage, especially when it comes to preventable ones. If you find yourself in a situation with multiple preventable failures, you need to reassess whether or not you're on the right path—something inside you might be trying to deliver the message that you don't really want to continue.

KNOW THYSELF

What is failure other than readjustments on our journey to success, your own scientific experiment in innovation and practice? It is during these readjustments that we best learn about ourselves and who we are; they give us the life experiences that allow us to improve and to help others.

A high level of self-awareness is required, then, to prevent unnecessary recurrences of failure. Self-awareness goes hand-in-hand with a certain amount of self-sufficiency and self-reliance, especially when you don't have a support system of people whose wisdom you trust—or if you're functioning without that support system for the first time in your life.

The threat of failure is frightening—believe me, I know. While failures aren't good experiences in general, they can be extremely useful. What comes from challenge and change? Growth. What comes from avoidance and stagnancy? Death—or something like it.

Failure is part of how we learn where our strengths lie and where they don't—how else would I have known I wasn't good at basketball if I hadn't tried and failed to make the team? But in trying out, I learned the truth, and as my parents would say, I made some adjustments to my new reality. In doing so, I used that "failure" as a way to increase my self-awareness and better define my path.

LESSON

Let failure become part of your filtering system.
It will help you learn where you should focus your energy.

KNOW THY ALLIES

You're not alone as you tackle new things, and sometimes the best thing you can do is ask for help along the way—or accept the wisdom and recognition of people we know are our allies. There's a reason you want to have someone you really trust with you when you try on clothes; you need someone you know will be honest with you when you come out of that dressing room.

For me, my first, greatest, and forever allies are my parents, and they were there for me in the best way during my foray into basketball. I knew my father would support me in trying out, because he loved the game, but I also trusted them to help me regain perspective when things didn't turn out the way I'd hoped.

Without their wise counsel, I might have wasted more time than I could afford on a detour from my true path to success.

Sometimes, we can't recognize our own failures for what they are, and that's when we need our allies to lend their perspective. However, it can be difficult to identify allies who help to focus you on your path versus deterrents who keep you from your true path.

Consider these questions:

- → Is this person invested in you and your success, and to what extent does their investment reach?
- → Have they demonstrated that they want you to succeed?
- → Have they been a helpful hand in the past?
- → Do they support and encourage you, even when you're not at your best?
- → Do they provide you with long-term perspective and truth, even if it may hurt your feelings in the short term and present?

If the answers to these questions are yes, then you have a true ally, and this is the kind of person who will be there for you and help you fail upward.

LEARNING FROM FAILURE

Failure is a tool that helps you refine your journey. We can learn best from failure if we stay humble and demonstrate the humility to accept it and gain wisdom from it, while embracing change and asking for help from our allies. Failure is painful, but it doesn't have to be damaging—and it doesn't have to be the end of a journey unless you know in your heart that's the right move.

When faced with failure, use your problem-solving tools to determine the type of failure and diagnose it, just like you might a patient: analyze the evidence and assess the root cause. Remember to look inwardly to yourself and outwardly at your environment to fully grasp the situation. Once you know the variables, you'll know better how to handle the failure and how it might be fixed, avoided, and prevented from recurring.

Failure is not a blame game, however. Rather, failure presents an opportunity to strategize for success. It should never be considered your friend, though, and you should never grow comfortable in its presence; instead, you should exploit failure and use it as a platform and opportunity to level-up.

To paraphrase my parents, be ready to adjust and recalculate, but don't be afraid to attempt something new just because you might fail. Take it from someone who was expected to fail at multiple points in her life, to the point that several people (not allies) attempted to deny me even the opportunity to take the risks necessary to achieve my goals.

I've heard the word *no* in my academic and professional life more times than I can count, enough times that hearing that word now just makes me smile, as it should you.

5

MY FIRST NO

In my second semester of my freshman year of college, I secured the meeting-of-all-meetings with a potential advisor I hoped would become a mentor on my path to medical school.

As the head of the psychobiology department, Dr. Nobriga was widely considered to be the most influential professor for anyone planning to go into medicine—for that alone, I wanted to impress her. However, I also admired her on a personal level. She was a refined and beautiful woman who wore her salt-and-pepper hair in a chic bob; everyone was drawn to her.

All the students agreed: if Dr. Nobriga signed off on you and agreed to be your advisor, you were good for the rest of your undergraduate career. You were *in*.

That day, while I sat across from Dr. Nobriga in her office, I waited with excitement as she reviewed my information. While I was nervous, I wasn't overly worried about my grades—I had finished my first semester with all *A*s except one *B+* in biology. That *B+* irked me, but I was still proud of my work.

My thoughts all centered on a common theme: *Please want to be my mentor.*

Dr. Nobriga's approval had become a cornerstone of my plans moving forward. I was convinced that if this one influential person was on my team, then my goal of becoming a doctor would be that much closer to succeeding, so I needed her on my team. I'd always been great at networking, having gained and maintained social capital at my school, so I was confident this meeting would pay off.

Although I didn't know it at the time, I was channeling my five-year-old naiveté at the church's national conference from all those years ago. I stepped on the stage, ready to be a star—only to be brought right back down to earth.

This time, however, instead of crickets from the audience, it was Dr. Nobriga's calm pronouncement: "Well, with these grades, I don't think you're going to get into medical school."

I'm fairly certain my entire body went numb at that point while she continued to speak. "Pre-med students really need to be getting straight *As*, especially in science courses. Looking at your transcript, that really doesn't bode well for you," she said.

Then she added, "Minorities, however, do very well in health psychology."

Whoa.

You know that part on the roller coaster where you start the free-fall from the top of the first peak and your heart just drops? That's all I could feel just then. The world went black for what seemed like an eternity. In reality, it took only about five seconds to completely process what I'd just been told.

For the first time in the history of my life, all of eighteen years at that point, someone told me I could not be a doctor. The pain of that dismissal, especially from someone in a position of power whom I admired, stayed with me for a long time afterward. In fact, thinking about it still stings.

You already know my dream of becoming a doctor has a happy ending, but in that moment I had my first truly impactful *no*—the first one with the potential to be a true dream-killer.

"Can you tell me more?" I asked, once I processed her words. Being painfully aware of this woman's position of power, I couldn't manage to say anything else. I needed to remain pleasant and not be viewed as aggressive or irrational, so I had to respond politely—even though my insides were churning. I was hurt, frustrated, and angry for so many reasons. After the comment about *minorities* doing better in health psychology, I'm not sure I actually heard anything else she said.

When my meeting with Dr. Nobriga was over, I left her office knowing I would never go back to her for advice. She would never sign off on any of my classes, or have any say in my undergraduate career…and I wasn't going to take her no as an answer to any questions I had about my future. I would simply maneuver around her *no* until I carved out my own *yes.*

LESSON

When people or situations tell you no, simply maneuver around it and strategize your yes.

DREAM-KILLER GONE VIRAL

While a perfect GPA is absolutely a benefit to any aspiring medical student, it's not a requirement. At least a 3.75 GPA is recommended, but there are many other factors involved in a medical school application, including extracurriculars, leadership experience, and volunteer work—not to mention MCAT scores and admissions essays. In fact, today, many medical schools and universities no longer rely on the GPA system. The essays give the applicants the opportunity to explain their reasons for wanting to become doctors, which reveals more about the person applying. Whether or not Dr. Nobriga believed I was qualified, I knew I was.

After graduation, I ended up connecting with Dr. Nobriga on social media. Years later, on June 16, 2017—the day I finished my Hand and Upper Extremity Surgical Fellowship—I was getting my hair done in preparation for the fellowship graduation. As you can imagine, I was very emotional. I'd just completed all my training—four years of undergraduate, four years of medical school, five years of orthopaedic surgery, and one year of fellowship training—as the first Black person to graduate from the fellowship program and the second Black person to graduate from the orthopaedic residency. A lifetime of work toward my goal.

I wrote a post about what had happened with Dr. Nobriga, and in it, I mentioned how children are encouraged to dream big until they get older, where the reality of success versus failure is more apparent. The closer you get to accomplishing your dreams, the easier it is for people to discourage you and marginalize your goals. Wrapping the post with a comment about how damaging it might have been to my future if I'd internalized what she'd said to me, I tagged her—not because I wanted to shame her, but because I wanted her to know how her comments had affected me, now that I felt free to say so. I had no way of knowing my post would go viral and reach tens of thousands of people.

First and foremost, I gained some closure on that episode in my life, because Dr. Nobriga actually reached out to me via Facebook Messenger. She said she didn't remember our encounter occurring that way, to which I said, "How could you? I was one of thousands of students who came to meet with you over the years."

More distressingly, however, about five people contacted me to tell me how Dr. Nobriga had given them similar advice—and they were all Black women. Every one of them said something akin to, "I'm so glad you succeeded, because I can only imagine where I might have been today. If I hadn't listened to her, I would have been a doctor."

I grieved for those women's dreams, killed by a person in a position of power and authority. If I hadn't been so focused and so determined to take on every challenge, I might have ended up the same way. Instead, Dr. Nobriga's *no* was a deal-breaker for any complacency I might have had up to that point. I filed her doubt away, put it in the back of my mind, and I kept going forward, because my Nanny and people like her needed me to.

I couldn't let the negative forces shape my future and forward progression. Dr. Nobriga may have doubted me, but I did not doubt myself.

That was the *real* challenge—and I accepted it.

A DREAM DEFERRED

When you're five and you say, "I want to be a doctor when I grow up," everyone encourages you. "Yes, you are," they say. "You can do it!" You'd have to be a really evil person to cock a brow and say, "Really?" and crush a kindergartener's dream. It's so far into the child's future... who's to say otherwise?

As you get older, however, the responses start to shift. When a middle schooler says, "I'm going to be a doctor," people still say, "You can do it," but they might add things like, "Gotta keep those grades up, though." Once you're in high school, the focus turns to not just grades but also opportunity: "Sure, if you can get scholarships," or "As long as you get into the right college."

And this is from your support system, those who are there to encourage you. Be mindful that they are also there to remind you of the realities of your situation.

People outside your support system will be supportive early on, but depending on your situation and their personality, you'll get more skepticism and outright disbelief as time marches on.

LESSON

Unfortunately, the closer you get to accomplishing your dreams, the easier it is for people to discourage you and marginalize your goals.

Many people don't get to live their dreams, so their lives may have fallen short of their goals—they may look at you and see a mirror of themselves: someone else who is destined to fail. Other people will judge you using metrics based on suppositions about who you are and what you can do. In general, many people have a tendency to superimpose their own failures, biases, and judgments onto others.

I'm pretty sure Dr. Nobriga had seen plenty of students who look like me not get into medical school, so she generalized and put that label onto me too.

What she said to me that day came from a place that had little to do with me not being a straight-*A* student. She had no way of understanding the foundation of where I was coming from, and my personal drive to accomplish my goals—the way my Nanny died because there wasn't a doctor who looked like me or talked like me to help her. When someone in a position of power tells you no, remember that at some point you too will be in a position to mentor students and encourage them. Instead of starting with no, finish with, "How can I help you get there?"

ARE YOU CAPABLE?

In some ways, I was lucky my experience with Dr. Nobriga was my first major obstacle. It was a wake-up call and a reminder of what the world tells little Black girls every day. Thank goodness it wasn't the devastating blow to my future it might have been.

I knew myself well enough to have a handle on what I could achieve and what was beyond my reach. When I think about self-awareness in terms of knowing yourself and what you can do, I think in terms of capabilities:

→ *What are your strengths?*

→ *What are your weaknesses?*

- *How do you react to pressure?*
- *How do you deal with stress?*
- *How do you deal with criticism?*

I knew those things about myself by age eighteen. While I had graduated at the top of my class in high school, I knew that may not happen while attending the University of Miami. I would be a diligent, hard-working student, but realistically, I was prepared to encounter students who were smarter and more academically gifted. Regardless, I was determined to make my grades what they needed to be, and I put my best efforts forth daily.

To that end, I knew certain classes were going to be more difficult for me than others. I had always struggled in chemistry, so when it was time to tackle those classes, I armed myself accordingly. My good fortune landed me a college roommate who happened to be awesome at organic chemistry, so I studied with her, asking questions upon questions to gain better understanding. Thankfully, she was patient enough to help me. One of the key strategies to success was to always surround myself with individuals smarter than me in arenas where I was weaker. In the words of Andrew Carnegie: "Never be so foolish as not to surround yourself with people who are smarter than you."

Was I a failure because some of these elements of my education weren't easy for me, or because other people did better in those arenas? No. Remember, failures can be motivators—any time I failed a test or an assignment, I came right back to pick my grades up again, getting help when I needed it. I didn't let those failures sink me, because I didn't let them keep me from getting to the next step. I learned from those failures, made adjustments, and kept going. You persevere, learn more about yourself, forgive yourself, and move forward.

As a scholar, I knew I was capable. Though it remained to be seen whether I was going to be *A*-, *B*-, or *C*-capable as a medical student, I knew I was capable of doing the academic work required. Though I did not ultimately predict that I would go into orthopaedic surgery, I knew myself well enough to know I was capable of it—or any surgical specialty. If I had failed to get into medical school, that would be one thing. But I didn't.

We have already learned the importance of self-awareness and how it evolves over time. If you choose to set off on an important journey, you have to know the basics of who you are, along with a strong, realistic sense of your own skills and abilities. Self-awareness informs your decisions along the way.

SEEK OUT WISE COUNSEL

While "know thyself" is evergreen advice, "no man is an island" stands as a well-known axiom for good reason. Everyone needs counselors, advisors, and mentors to help them navigate all the points on their path to success. This is a fact.

It's also a fact, however, that not every person in a position to advise or mentor you will be the best person for that role—for a variety of reasons. So, how will you know who is giving you wise counsel suited to your goals and capabilities and who isn't?

Many people may be willing to offer you counsel, but are they wise enough—and frankly, *worthy* enough—to do so? Do they know *you*, or are they trying to shove you into a template based on generalizations and assumptions?

In many ways, we tend to let others define our failures for us—or, more accurately, we let them set us up to accept those perceived failures as the end of some part of our journey. This is often presented as a good thing: *Have you considered health psychology? It's great! It even pays really well!* The end of the journey may be made to look inviting, nicely wrapped in pretty paper, but if it is the wrong advice, something that causes you to stop and step down from what could be true greatness, it's no gift. At best, it's a consolation prize—at worst, a tragedy.

This was the impression I got from the emails of those women who shared their experiences with Dr. Nobriga after my post went viral. These women had listened to what they thought was wise counsel and instead made a tragic mistake: they'd let someone else stop them from continuing their journey to medical school. They are successful in their current careers, but they are not passionate about what they are doing. It wasn't who they were. They allowed someone to tell them no, and they accepted that negative advice and chose an alternative path.

I realized early in the game it was best to find advisors who had a journey that mirrored mine, or at least *understood* the journey I was on. Dr. Nobriga was an excellent advisor for other students, many of whom still sing her praises today. She may have been the head of the department, but she was the worst possible advisor for someone like me, just as she was for those women.

Any time you open yourself up to guidance from someone you don't already know or trust, you're taking a chance. But there are steps you can take to protect yourself.

As I progressed in my academic career, I gave myself permission to think critically and selectively about the authority figures I looked to for advice and mentorship. I researched them and their backgrounds, found out more about how they applied their knowledge and experience to guide others. In short, I vetted them to the best of my abilities.

But if I'm being honest, the bare facts alone didn't determine whose opinions and suggestions I trusted. Being proactive with research is smart, but every time I found myself in an introductory meeting with a potential mentor, my gut instincts about that person cast the deciding vote.

If you do the research and actively look for the wise counsel you need, you'll be prepared—but your gut will do the rest. Wise counsel requires supportive acknowledgment of your goal, a realistic assessment, and a willingness to help. You know you've found the right person if they say something akin to, "The path you're on is a difficult one. Let me give you some tools that will benefit you along the way. I can't guarantee you'll succeed, but I believe in you."

That's what it looks like. That's wise counsel, delivered with care, generosity, humility, and passion.

If an otherwise reputable and wise person tries to direct you off your path, even though you know it's within your capabilities—or worse, tells you something that devastates you on a personal level—only you can determine how to deal with their words.

But thanks to Dr. Nobriga, I have a tool for that. I always tell my mentees, "When you get hit with something hard, take about five to ten seconds to digest it. Then move forward; persevere."

Sometimes, moving forward might mean removing that advisor from your team. Don't be afraid to walk out of that meeting without a backward glance—even if they are head of their department. In the words of my Jamaican grandfather, "Always move forward, never look backward."

Staying Humble

As you already know, I didn't alter my path after that meeting with Dr. Nobriga. I completed my bachelor's degree, stayed on the premed track, took the MCAT, and went on to medical school—and I was never a straight-*A* student. Every time I heard *no* along the way, I let it go in one ear and out the other.

This is why I'm always going to advocate for strength in the face of adversity. When someone tells you no, you say, "Challenge accepted."

Sometimes, I still think about Dr. Nobriga messaging me and telling me she didn't remember our meeting the same way I did. I think it goes deeper than that: she had no idea of the impact of her words.

As you achieve success along your journey, you'll have to be both a receiver of advice and a giver of advice. Now that I've had a chance to be a mentor to others who are seeking to be doctors, I can see firsthand the importance of making sure I choose my advice carefully, making sure I'm delivering the most balanced wisdom I can.

The most difficult part has been situations in which I have to deliver a *no* to someone who has the dream but neither the drive nor the capabilities to continue their journey into medical school or orthopaedics. I remember each one well, because there have only been three. For each of those three people, I considered the situation from every possible angle and tried to ensure I wasn't their dream-killer.

In each case, I shared with them my experience with Dr. Nobriga. I told them I didn't think this path was for them, but as I explained why, I still gave them the tools they could use to prove me wrong. The best part is one of those three people ended up doing just that. She accepted the challenge—and I've never been so proud to have been wrong about something!

Humility opens your understanding of the power locked into that moment. Knowing what it did to me, I know what it could do to them, so this puts the impetus on me to remember. Humility should guide what we say and how we say it, understanding the impact it will make on others.

When we let other people define or set up our perceived failures, we also let them set the standards for our successes. This to our own detriment. We should set our own standards on the journey instead of giving that power away. When you set the standard, you can gauge the success, and it makes all the difference.

6

MATCHING UP

Confession time: When I began my studies at Morehouse School of Medicine, I had never heard of an orthopaedic surgeon.

Then, in my first year of medical school, a compelling Black woman, an orthopaedic surgeon, walked into the lecture hall to give a presentation on the subject to my class.

While the presentation on orthopaedics was fascinating, I was even more intrigued by the surgeon herself, Dr. Bonnie Simpson Mason. Beautiful and self-assured, she moved like she was always aware of the space around her; she spoke with poise and eloquence.

Had I been a cartoon character, there would have been stars in my eyes. I was literally looking at the kind of woman I wanted to become. There are two slides I remember from that presentation: how to draw the brachial plexus, and the last slide, which stated, "Only the top 5 percent of the class will successfully match into orthopaedics."

I stared at that slide and thought, *Wow. So that's what it takes.* My GPA was not "top 5 percent" material, nor was it likely to become so. Yet there was not a doubt in my mind that I was capable of becoming an orthopaedic surgeon.

LESSON

Never tell yourself that you are incapable of accomplishing a goal.

After the presentation, we went into a bone lab to get hands-on experience on setting fractures using plates and pins. The experience was intense. At one of the lab stations, I fumbled with a lobster-claw clamp—a tool that holds the bone together—while working on a fractured synthetic bone.

"Wow, this is kind of awkward," I said wryly to the orthopaedic surgeon working with me at the lab station. The surgeon, a Black man, slanted me a solemn look.

"There's not enough people who look like you in this field," he said. "So if you're serious about this, you better learn how to handle it."

I took a breath, steadied myself, and tried again.

That day was my first real experience with orthopaedics. I'd seen the challenge and the rigor involved, both academically and practically…and unbeknownst to me at that time, I'd also seen a glimpse of my future.

"You Look Like an Orthopaedic Surgeon"

I had spent my second year of medical school continuing my studies on the path to becoming a surgeon. I became president of the James Densler Surgical Society and secured mentors in the field of general surgery. You may have noticed that I haven't mentioned orthopaedic surgery; that may be due to a few stumbling blocks that occurred after my initial excitement for the orthopaedic lecture given by Dr. Simpson Mason.

First, I was discouraged from entering the field by several attendings at the medical school, attendings who I honestly respected and whose lack of approval of the field was not fueled by lack of belief that I would be successful but rather their knowledge of the rareness of Black women in the field. Second, there was a program aimed to introduce minority students to the field of orthopaedic surgery. I applied, I was excited, and I was not accepted! So, expectedly, my passion for orthopaedics faded, but did not disappear. Yet another lesson in perseverance.

In spring of my third year, I earned a scholarship to attend the Student National Medical Association (SNMA). I was leaning toward a future in general surgery. I had the support of general surgery mentors, and I was president of the student surgical society. Yet I felt as if I was telling myself no to the field of orthopaedic surgery.

While attending the SNMA conference that year, I happened to walk past a table where two orthopaedic surgeons stood: Dr. Erica Taylor (now Erica Taylor-Webb), then a third-year resident, and Dr. Toni McLaurin, a trauma surgeon—both Black women. Dr. McLaurin especially was something of a rockstar to me, as she was only the second Black female orthopaedic surgeon I'd met after Dr. Mason.

As I glided past them, my gaze lingered.

"Hey! You look like an orthopaedic surgeon!" one of them called out. Embarrassed but a little pleased, I laughed and moved toward them.

"Um, *what*?"

"Oh, yeah," Erica said. After she gave me the elevator speech about how well her residency was going, she concluded, "You should really look into orthopaedics."

Now it was Dr. McLaurin's turn. "We're hosting a breakout group tomorrow for people interested in orthopaedics," she smiled. "Are you interested?"

My heart gave a little lurch. In a flash, I remembered Dr. Mason, and the way I had felt, watching her presentation.

"Tell me the time and place," I said, smiling back. "I'll be there fifteen minutes early."

Dr. McLaurin laughed. "Oh, you're *definitely* an orthopaedic surgeon!"

I walked away with a new spring in my step and a growing conviction that I had found my true path. The breakout group clinched it.

By the end of the conference, I had made the decision to switch my planned specialty to orthopaedic surgery. As luck would have it, I ran into Dr. Mason before the end of the conference. It was April 2—my birthday.

I held back for a nanosecond, wondering if I should approach her, right then and there. I've never been one for waiting, and besides, it was my birthday.

"Dr. Mason," I said, walking over to her. "Do you have a minute?"

I poured out my new plan while she listened, patiently. "I know it's April, and we're choosing our fourth year rotations in a few months, but..." I took a deep breath "...I'm deciding *now* that I want to be an orthopaedic surgeon. What do I need to do?"

Dr. Mason didn't bat an eye. We sat down together, and she helped me plot out a whole new course of action for the rest of my medical school career. I would have to cram a whole year's worth of work into a short period of time; that was the only way to prepare for the rotations I would need to match into orthopaedics.

I went back to Morehouse with a new sense of purpose, so excited I could barely contain it: *I'm going to be an orthopaedic surgeon! I found my specialty!*

Then, reality made a crash landing. As I began working out the logistics, I could see all the mountains and valleys I would have to forge. I would need new letters of recommendation, and I had to scrap my original rotation applications for general surgery.

Morehouse didn't have an orthopaedic program, so I would have to do every "away rotation" without a trial run at my home base. Rotations in orthopaedic surgery were available, but they were highly competitive. My scores weren't even high enough to qualify for all of them, and those programs were scattered all around the country.

My God, how am I going to be able to pay to go to these rotations? I thought, beginning to panic. Unable to process it all, I called Dr. Mason, hoping for a sympathetic ear.

What I got, instead, was the wake-up call of a lifetime.

"Lattisha..." she began. Her voice was kind, but firm. "Piss, or get off the pot."

Without another word, she hung up the phone. That was all I needed to realize that the bridge between reality and dreams is *work fueled by grit.* I would have to put in the work to make the dream a reality. Dr. Mason very bluntly reminded me that I had stated what I intended to do, so it was up to me to make it happen. The only other option—the easier option—was to give up and get out of the way.

Throughout my higher education, my father had offered similar advice. As I agonized over getting into medical school or applying for programs, he would say, "Hey, do you want to be a doctor? Then do it."

Sometimes, it's as simple as that.

ON ROTATION

I have talked quite a bit about my grandfather walking off the boat in England with nothing but one suitcase and a name on a piece of paper. He was materially underequipped, so he had to rely on his intelligence and ability to adapt.

Never in my life have I felt his spirit quite as keenly as I did when I started my orthopaedic rotations—because I was not fully prepared. Unlike every other medical student I met at the start of my fourth year, I hadn't been exactly laser-focused on orthopaedics during my academic career. My education had been thorough, so I knew the basics, but I didn't know the lingo or the atmosphere or the bravado that often accompanies students rotating in orthopaedic surgery. On some level, I understood the culture shock that my grandfather experienced. I resolved to persevere.

Although I should have expected it, I had not banked on orthopaedics being a distinctly White, male-dominated sphere—with all the bravado and macho behavior that goes along with it. I'd logged important face-to-face time with three Black women orthopaedic surgeons who inspired me to start the journey, and who gave me a chance to follow them. Now I was in a position to take my shot, but it was up to me not to blow it.

There was no point in pretending I knew everything about orthopaedics when I didn't. I buckled down to do the work. Sometimes it was humbling, especially in the beginning, but I learned not to be ashamed to ask, *What is that?* or *What does that mean?* It was the only way to get my knowledge base onto the same level as my peers.

I also learned to stay true to who I was, despite pressure to join in with the crowd. I have never been a drinker or a partier, and so many of the other folks on rotation were. Instead of closing down the bar, I would go out with them, have my glass of wine, and go home. I got teased for it—some things never change—but I have never regretted those choices. I wasn't there to socialize or hook up; I was there on a mission. I made a few friends along the way who are now practicing orthopaedic surgeons too. Unfortunately, I also ran up against misogyny and sexual harassment during my first away orthopaedic rotation.

Mid-procedure while performing a hip replacement, the attending surgeon stopped and looked at me.

"Hey, can I trust you?"

I was observing him perform a type of surgery I'd never seen before. I watched everything he did, trying to learn it all, so when the surgeon stopped and asked me that question, it was a surprise.

"Um..." I began.

"Yes or no," he said, "but can I really trust you?"

Confused, I nodded and said, "Yes, sir." How else was I supposed to respond in this environment?

My confusion turned to nausea when the surgeon, in all seriousness, told me that the chief resident had been spreading a rumor that he and I were sleeping together. "He told me you let him hit that," he said, with a ghost of a smirk.

All I could manage between the sick feeling in my stomach and the mortification flooding my body was to say, "No, sir. That never happened."

Without missing a beat, the surgeon looked back down at the patient and pointed to an area in the hip. "What muscle is responsible for the external rotation of the hip?"

Gut-punch. Was he serious? Talk about setting someone up for failure! With his disgusting tale still ringing in my ears—*he told me you let him hit that*—I blanked, and what came out of my mouth was the exact wrong answer. My shame metastasized even before he shook his head, as if I were a pitiful excuse for a wannabe doctor.

"I would never accept you into this program," he said. "You're never going to match into orthopaedics."

The hits just kept on coming. During my rotations and the intensive interview process in that fourth year, I privately broke down in tears twice because of negativity like this. It wasn't just the sexual harassment or the spiteful gossip; it was everyone saying *no, no, no.*

It was up to me to keep faith in myself and find my *yes.*

Piss or get off the pot, Lattisha. Above all else, persevere.

MAKE ME A MATCH

Have you ever found yourself running from store to store in a time crunch, trying desperately to find one specific thing you need to make a plan work?

This was how the morning of the most important interview of my medical school career began.

Early on in the interview process, I'd tried to hedge my bets. My friends and advisors in medical school urged me to interview for general surgery and orthopaedics, just in case the latter didn't work out. After my second general surgery interview, however, I canceled the rest, much to their horror. I could not have a safety net and still devote all my energy to my true goal.

LESSON

When you truly believe in yourself, it's best to go all-in.

If I had learned anything in my lifetime, from my grandparents and my parents, it was to never settle for something you don't really want just because it might be easier. For me, it was orthopaedics or nothing.

When I secured an interview at the University of Texas Medical Branch in Galveston, Texas—the oldest orthopaedic program in that state—I was bubbling over with excitement. I arrived at my hotel late Friday night and unpacked my clothes, getting everything out so I would be ready to leave early in the morning for my interview. Everything was running on schedule.

When I took out my suit for the interview, however, I was crushed. My suit jacket wasn't there. I felt my heart beating into my throat, and my face grew hot and sweaty. *What to do, what to do…*

Orthopaedics is competitive. It's conservative. I could not show up wearing dress pants and a blouse—that would mean failing my interview before it even began.

I have always taken great pride in my ability to persevere and plan, but I still had my scatterbrained moments. Had I gone through my things the day before, I would have found and fixed the problem *before* it was a problem.

Now I was in a different state, with fifty dollars on my debit card, and it was 11:00 p.m. Nothing was open, not even in other towns nearby.

Panic set in, but there was no time for that, so I shifted gears. Lattisha, get it together. Failure is not an option. What are your choices?

I could call and try to push back my interview, but that isn't who I am.

I could go to my interview without a jacket, but it would show my lack of planning.

I could show up early, ready to go, without making excuses for myself. That's who I am.

The interview was at 8:00 a.m., so I got up hours beforehand. There were three Walmarts between me and my interview—the only clothing store open at that hour—so I hit them all. Walmart isn't exactly known for its business wear, however, and I didn't find anything like a suit jacket until I reached the third store.

I found a blazer that would work. It was a few sizes too big, but it would work.

So I put on that giant blazer and told myself to be confident. *Carry yourself with distinction,* I reminded myself. *Confidence lifts you up. If you don't act like you're a little girl wearing her mother's jacket, they won't see you that way.*

I walked into that room wearing my oversized blazer, and surveyed the other applicants just as they did me. Plenty of cowboy boots, which would have been ridiculous if they were at an interview in New York or Los Angeles, but this was Texas.

I was the only Black woman in the room.

If they can get away with wearing cowboy boots, I reasoned, *then my giant blazer will be just fine.*

And it was. I matched into their orthopaedics program, the second Black woman to do so in its history.

I still have that oversized Walmart blazer. I'll never be able to part with it, because it was part of what resulted in my first major victory in the field of orthopaedics.

ILLEGITIMI NON CARBORUNDUM

No one expected me to match into orthopaedics because I didn't fit society's mold of what an orthopaedic surgeon should be. I wasn't an athletic, six-foot-tall White guy whose father was an orthopaedic surgeon too. That was okay, though, because I had seen what orthopaedic surgeons looked like, and I knew they could and did look like me.

Throughout my post-secondary academic—undergraduate and medical school—one of the most important tools I learned was to filter out what I call *white noise* while you're working to achieve a goal.

White noise might be other people's successes or failures; it might be what other people say about you; it might be the labels or standards put on you by others. Whatever form it takes, white noise is just that: noise. You can't submit to other people's standards of success or perceptions of you.

LESSON

If you set the standard, then you also gauge your success.

If I had listened to that surgeon during my first rotation—if I'd internalized his sexual harassment and his scornful pronouncement that I'd never match into orthopaedics—I might have given up. Instead, he taught me a valuable lesson: if you don't know who you are, you're always going to be vulnerable to the labels people put on you. Granted, I left that encounter shaken, but not defeated. I was going to match, but not into his program. That was fine with me. At that point, I wouldn't have accepted an invitation to join his orthopaedic program, even if it was the last one on earth.

He tried to take power from me, but I didn't let him—and I was the only one who could give him the ability to hurt me. Yes, early on I did not know as much about orthopaedics as the other students, but he was trying to prey on my weakness, which was clear to everyone in those early rotations. That said, I refused to be ashamed of what I didn't know, because it drove me to work hard every second of every day to catch up.

Never be ashamed to ask a question. If you are ill-equipped for the goal you've chosen, it is up to you to equip yourself—and to use the tools you already have to help you do so. You can make up for a lack of information with passion and eagerness to learn in every way possible. I keep that humility with me to this day, thanks to those early orthopaedic rotations.

Just like everything else in life, if you don't actively pursue what you want, you won't get it—and that includes acquiring information. You have to push forward, always, no matter who or what is trying to hold you back.

We can get bogged down in our fears and worries, but there comes a time when you have to piss or get off the pot, just as my mentor said that to me at a crucial point in my life. I now use that bit of wisdom with my own mentees. When they start showing signs of wobbling, saying things like, "I don't know if I can do this," I go full-on Dr. Mason: "Well, then, go find something else. Piss or get off the pot."

If they want it badly enough, they suck it up and find a way. They find the inspiration and mentorship they need in others who came before them, like I did with Drs. Mason, Taylor-Webb, and McLaurin. They take the negative experiences along the way and use them as fuel. They take that vision of the future and figure out the logistics of making it their reality.

LESSON

Perseverance may not be a marathon,

but your life goals are.

Your only real competitor is *you*.

It's up to you to step forward and put the work in, to advocate for yourself, and to ensure your success. If you equip yourself with that kind of work ethic early on, you'll be ready not only for the marathon but for all those sprints along the way.

You probably already know that making your dreams a reality will be an ongoing fight. I am here to tell you that it's not the war that wears you down. It's all those little battles that cause conflict every day that can eat you up from the inside if you let them… Persevere, regardless.

7

AWKWARD . . . OR STYLISH?

The next time you hold a pen or pencil to write something, take a moment to observe the way you hold it: the placement of your middle and index finger, the angle of your wrist, the slant of your forearm.

Then, when you get an opportunity, look at how other people hold their pen or pencil. Even if it's similar, it's not quite the same—right? And while you might think their way of holding that writing utensil is weird, you have to remember that it works for them—just like the way you hold it works for you. Everyone has their own style when it comes to using physical tools.

Even surgeons.

The five years of my residency were the most grueling years of my entire journey to becoming an orthopaedic surgeon. I don't say that lightly, because nothing about becoming a doctor is easy. It wasn't just the long hours or the amount of work residents have to put in; those elements are to be expected. I was there to learn how to become a surgeon, and the attending surgeons and chief residents were there to teach me. Those years of on-the-job training served a crucial purpose in practicing all the skills I had learned, safely, on actual patients. I couldn't have started my own practice without them.

While I came into my residency excited to begin practicing medicine, I also found myself in a whole new world of being judged by others. Having your every move observed and examined by multiple sets of eyes, day in, day out, can be exhausting, especially when their evaluations of you and your work aren't always balanced, fair, or actively useful. And because of who I was—not only an aspiring surgeon, but also a young Black woman—I found myself scrutinized and called out for everything from my name, to my clothes, to how I held my surgical tools.

Case in point: after watching me perform a successful partial hip-replacement, my attending surgeon told me afterward, "You operate awkwardly."

Um, what?

I tried to absorb those words, but I just couldn't for a moment. Worse yet, this wasn't a mandatory meeting; I had initiated it myself. Seeking out my attendings for weekly evaluations on my surgeries felt like the best way to improve my skills and to keep myself up to speed on how I was being evaluated along the way.

Of course, certain personal biases and subjectivity could often be seen in those evaluations, but this note in particular struck me as so vague, it went beyond subjective commentary and into outright personal preference.

It reverberated in my head: "You operate awkwardly." How was I supposed to respond to that? Thank you, sir. Now, how do I do it ...not awkwardly?

After that brief pause, I asked the attending if he could give more feedback about the core elements of the surgery. I listed out some basic fundamentals: appropriate surgical time, no complications, blood loss minimal, patient recovered well. Post-operatively, the hip components were appropriately aligned on X-ray imaging, while the incision was closed without tension.

All of this information felt very positive, but we still hadn't talked about the elephant in the room. "But the surgery was... awkward?"

I was trying to understand him, asking as politely as possible, even though I just wanted to demand, *Can you define awkward? I can't write down "be less awkward." I don't know how to improve that, or even how to try improving that.*

"It's more the way you hold the tools," he said. By this point, we were both becoming uncomfortable. "It looks awkward."

Just like that, I knew what he meant.

I didn't "operate awkwardly." I just didn't operate like *he* did, because in surgery, as in life, I was developing my own style.

THE ELEMENTS OF STYLE

When it comes to operative technique, there are certain points that are essential for the success of the surgery and in order to keep the patient's health at a premium during and after the procedure. When the surgery is successful and your patient not only survives but thrives afterward, the manner in which you hold a surgical tool is not as important as what occurs when you wield that tool in your hands. If you've performed many successful surgeries, it's obvious that how you operate isn't right or wrong in any measurable sense; it's your style, and it's how you do it.

I really wanted to say something akin to this during that evaluation:

Was the surgery successful? Yes.

Did the patient stay in surgery or recovery a minute longer than they might have if someone else operated? No.

So, I don't operate the way you do. I'll bet we hold our pens differently too.

And correct me if I'm wrong, but that particular surgery wasn't named after you, was it? Well, if you didn't invent it, then I'm going to assume you're not the gold standard for performing it.

Oh, it's a very good thing I didn't say any of *that*.

Even though I didn't realize it fully at the time, I was developing my own surgical style, independent of what I'd learned from books and observation. My style wasn't exactly like the doctors I had read about or had seen perform surgery many times, but I did incorporate elements from those individuals and reflected them in my own work.

When you are the only one who looks like you in the room—or, in my case, the second in the history of the orthopaedic program—people tend to scrutinize more deeply. They also often focus on those nonessential factors rather than the positive outcomes.

We can all write clearly with our pens, no matter how differently we might hold them. My surgeries were as successful as everyone else's, including that particular surgeon's—who, by the way, never told me I was awkward again.

My surgical style wasn't—and isn't—awkward. It's mine. I operate like Lattisha, and she's a damn good surgeon. When developing my own style, I took the following steps:

1. Study and replicate the foundation of a technique.
2. Model that technique after those with years of experience.
3. Develop your own style in a safe and reproducible manner.
4. Practice not until you get it right, but until you can't get it wrong.

(DON'T) BE AGGRESSIVE

During my years in residency, I was under constant scrutiny (sometimes appropriately, and other times not) from not only my attending surgeons, but also my peers. I was the second Black resident in the history of the program, I was not a Texas native, and I attended a medical school without an orthopaedic program.

As usual, there was no way to blend into the crowd, so I focused on distinguishing myself and building my social capital, just like my grandfather did.

I knew I was going to need allies in the program going forward, so I made sure that the senior residents knew who I was and that I was a go-getter with a solid work ethic. They might not always be able to have my back if I ran into problems, but at least they could stand up and speak favorably about me.

LESSON

Use your assets as a form of protection.

I also made sure to get to know the people I was working with. I made a point to socialize with the other residents outside the hospital, even if I was still just drinking my glass of wine and heading home earlier than most of the crowd.

Building social capital can only take you so far, however. While the majority of my peers and mentors were supportive, I experienced my share of racial and misogynistic aggression along the way.

One particular memory? My name. At the time, I wasn't married, so my full maiden name was Lattisha Latoyah Rowe.

I hadn't really internalized the implications of the ethnic spelling until the first day of an intern rotation, when a chief resident remarked, "Oh, I saw your name on the roster for the new interns. *Lattisha. Latoyah.* You've got to be trouble." He spoke in an exaggerated mimicry of ethnic, African-American vernacular. Say *what?*

My family had instilled so much pride in me regarding my name, I always used my full name any time a name was required—school registration, buying a vehicle, and so on. I considered it a badge of honor, and used it professionally too, making it part of my personal style. I never realized that it could be used as an insult until he said that to me. It's not like my name was Lucifer or Hitler; seems to me those names, or perhaps the parents who would name their children as such in modern times, would indicate far more trouble.

Worse, though, was the American-born Greek attending physician at an ICU rotation. He read out the roll of new people, and it was literally as simple and straightforward as, "Ryan Morris, welcome to the rotation. Susie Phillips, welcome to the rotation," until he got to my name.

"Lattisha Latoyah Rowe," he read aloud. Then he looked at me and said, in what I suppose he thought was his best Black-woman voice, "Oh, *girlfriend*, you better not be giving me no issues or problems," while he flicked his fingers and rolled his head from side to side. *Seriously?*

This man judged me, stereotyped me, and categorized me as a problem based merely on my name. The name that my parents proudly gave me twenty-five years before, the name that was read as I proudly crossed the stage while earning my medical degree. He was already creating a persona around me, a second-generation British-born woman of Jamaican heritage, from his preconceived notions.

Sometimes that's what happens when you are the only one like you in the room. Suddenly, you're working with people who haven't interacted with anyone who looks like you, who sounds like you, who has your background or your experiences. And the way they act toward you and respond to you can be intentionally aggressive, meant to belittle you, or simply uninformed—which means they're still reducing you to stereotypes. Take that opportunity to shift their paradigm and excel in the face of their ignorance.

THE STRUGGLE BUS

Aggression doesn't always come from those who perceive you as different, however.

I did a subspecialty rotation during my first second-year rotation that came very close to shifting the entire course of my career because I felt such an affinity for it. Unfortunately, one of the attendings who looked like me was also not too keen on me, or my style. *At all.*

I don't expect the entire world to love me, of course, but up until that point, my most important mentors had all been Black women working in my field. It hurt to know that someone whose approval was important to me had no interest in me, or my career.

Our first few days of working together during that rotation were uncomfortable—I felt a bit like a puppy who kept getting ignored or pushed aside by an older dog. Then, one day, she pulled me into her office. "I'd like to meet with you," she said, her tone too bland to signal her motivation.

Finally! I thought gleefully. *She wants to know more about me, or maybe she wants to share her story about how she became an orthopaedic surgeon, and how she excelled to where she is today.*

I followed her into her office and took a seat, bursting with excitement. *Maybe she'll offer to be my mentor. Maybe she'll ask me to think about coming to work with her!*

Instead, once she sat down behind her desk, she steepled her fingers and measured me with stern eyes. "Several of the PAs have been complaining about the way your hair smells," she announced.

"I'm—I'm sorry?" I said, trying to keep my voice from shaking. A gnawing pit of embarrassment opened in my stomach.

"Yes," she said. "We're just a little concerned about it."

So, she'd been talking to the PAs about me. I had to swallow down another blow to my pride on that one. I'd seen and heard her doing that kind of thing at various times. It was part of her personality to make fun of other students and even other attendings on a whim, though never to the point that anyone would complain or cite her for harassment; however, she had a subtle undertone of spite.

And now, I realized, I was the butt of one of her jokes.

The only way I could think to deal with this was to face it head on and try to make this a positive encounter. "Right," I said, keeping my voice level. "Well, I'm sorry about that. Do you have any suggestions for products to use, or a loctician you recommend?"

"I don't know," she said, leaning back in her chair. "It's your hair."

At that point, I would have done just about anything to get out of her office. "Well, I'll see what I can do," I managed. "Is there anything else you wanted to talk about?"

Her eyebrows drew together. *Oh, no.* "You know, you wear too much color to clinic," she said, looking pointedly at my red collared shirt. "When I was going through orthopaedics, it was white- and male-dominated. We wore gray, white, and black. Period."

While I was processing this, she added, "And the way you dress in general is inappropriate for this job."

I had a sudden flashback to a department gathering a few evenings earlier. I'd worn a pair of red feathered earrings, one of my favorites, and in front of everyone, this woman had said, "You look like you belong on an Indian reservation." They all laughed, while I wanted to sink into the floor. I thought that was just a one-time joke—not a persistent insult.

"You're busting out with red and orange, all these bright colors," she said, pinning me with a glare. "When you're an attending, you can do that. But you aren't there yet."

Her tone on the last part seemed to imply that *yet* might be *never*.

I left that office shaken to my core—this was different from my experience with Dr. Nobriga. By calling me out on my physical style, she made this personal: she was attacking aspects of my *person*. Had she been calling me out as blatantly unprofessional, it would be one thing, but I didn't dress unprofessionally; I just didn't dress the way *she thought I should.*

And why? Because she didn't like me? Because she didn't like the way I looked, acted...or *smelled*? I was firm in knowing my hair did not stink; my locs were (and always are) groomed, clean, and neat. Was there any discussion about lacking in knowledge or surgical proficiency as a junior resident? Not at all.

No, her animosity toward me ran deeper than that. Unlike my encounters with racism and misogyny, she wasn't aggressive toward me because I was different, but because I was *too much like her.*

She seemed to think I wasn't struggling as much as she had had to struggle while she was in her residency. That comment about how orthopaedics used to be male-dominated? It still was (still is), and she knew it. Things were opening up for Black women a little more all the time, however, and it burned her that, in her eyes, my path was easier than hers had been. Maybe a few more doors were open, and a few less hoops were required...but I still had to show up, walk through, and jump through. A few more opportunities may have been available, but *I still had to do the work.*

She didn't want me to fail. I firmly believe that. She wasn't throwing up obstacles for me. She also wasn't going to help me jump over any obstacles, though, especially in terms of moral support. I had jumped into the river, so to speak, by going into orthopaedics; if I swam, fine, but if I didn't, she wasn't going to throw me a life vest.

She wanted me to struggle because she had struggled. Period.

Needless to say, I didn't go into that subspecialty of orthopaedics, but this encounter turned out to be useful in other ways. This encounter was a reality check. There was some truth there, when it came to how I brought my style onto the job. But the most important thing I learned from her was to recognize her type quickly, and keep from investing in their good opinion, because it would be impossible to earn it.

IN STYLE WE TRUST

From all these experiences—plus all the others like them, which are probably too many to count—I've learned to remember who I am and stay true to my personal style. I would remind myself that the success of an award-winning novelist does not suffer because someone else simply doesn't like the way they hold their pen.

And I have to trust in myself, because like every other Black professional out there, I've had to work twice as hard and be twice as smart to be considered just as good as everyone else. I also had to learn to ask for help when I needed it, which may have been the hardest thing of all. Just because I trust in myself doesn't mean I do so blindly, when there are knowledgeable people all around me.

The disheartening thing about this particular experience is that too often, people will take the best parts of you and try to use them to engineer your downfall. But they can't succeed in such an endeavor unless you let them, so you have to adapt to what are valid suggestions while orchestrating yourself in a way that is intrinsic to who you are. Case in point: around that particular attending, I stuck with grays, whites, and blacks for my business attire, because I was still in a learning apprenticeship environment. For the remainder of my training, I continued to wear colors that are vibrant and represent my mood and style—a practice I continue to this day.

In the end, what saved me from self-doubt and got me past the obstacles was my work ethic and my willingness to go above and beyond in everything I do.

And I am still myself—mentally, physically, and stylistically—on the job. I do things my way and am proud to do so. I continue to evolve my style by absorbing the technique, wisdom, and style of those around me both in and out of the operating room.

Fast forward a decade or so from my training environment, I find myself in the position of having to speak to a resident or an intern about their personal dress. It's unavoidable; fashion changes, style changes, and expectations of professional dress have shifted. I think back to the way I wish that orthopaedic surgeon had talked to me, however, and I keep my remarks based in professionalism, truth, and kindness.

And instead of saying, "I don't know," when they ask what they can do better, I share what I know about hair care and dressing professionally—and I've been known to hand out money for a trip to the salon, or buy an intern a suit for interviews. I share expectations of dress based on where they may rotate or interview, pointing out the need to adhere to professional standards while maintaining their own sense of style.

The same philosophy applies when I deliver feedback on a surgery. I keep my comments actionable and objective, because I've never forgotten how I felt that day I was told my operating style was *awkward.*

Well, awkward or not, this is the way I hold the scalpel—and get great outcomes.

Throughout my career, I've been besieged by the perceptions of others. Sometimes those perceptions actualize as microaggressions, like the flak I've gotten about my name and its spelling. They also get expressed as outright hostility, sometimes targeting my appearance or my gender, other times targeting my progress, despite the odds.

It hasn't really stopped, even as I've become a practicing surgeon. I still get odd looks because of my style of dress or my style of locs—and, as I've mentioned before, I've been mistaken for the janitor or the delivery person when I'm in scrubs, or even wearing a white coat. That's a form of hostility too, aimed directly at my race: some people look at a Black person, especially a Black woman, in an operating room, and their first thought is, *Are you supposed to be here?*

Why yes, I am. Are *you*?

Keep yourself above the subjectivity and negativity. Yes, it can be tricky, but it's easier if you have like-minded company. Find others who want to keep themselves above the fray, and you'll have another important layer of support.

8

THE FELLOW IN PEARLS AND HEELS

If you watch medical TV shows, I'm sure you have noticed that surgeons generally wear comfortable shoes when they're in the operating room. There is a reason for that—if you are going to be on your feet, standing mostly in one place for hours at a time, you don't want to risk distractions from foot discomfort. You need flat shoes with good support.

I tend to wear Tory Burch loafers during procedures—they're both stylish and comfortable, and you know how I feel about style. There was one memorable time in my life, however, when circumstances put me in the operating room wearing heels, and that uncomfortable experience played a surprising role in determining the course of my fellowship year—which, in turn, led to an important milestone in my career.

As I neared the end of my residency, I realized I wanted to subspecialize in hand surgery, so I spent my final year as a resident interviewing for fellowships at the top hand surgery programs in the country.

The fellowship process works much like the match system—the applicant interviews with different programs, and both the applicant and program create rank lists to be matched up by a computer.

Of course, I approached the fellowship interviews with a wholly different mindset.

Five years earlier, I had been so intensely focused on matching into orthopaedics that the pressure was nearly overwhelming. This time, I approached the process with confidence. I had come such a long way and had accomplished so much already that I didn't doubt that I was going to get a fellowship—and I was going to get my top-choice program.

All the advice I had received so far was to rank my choices in terms of prestige, not comfort level. What constituted "top choice" for me, however, wasn't necessarily the actual program's notoriety; I had good interviews at the top-ranked hand programs in the nation, and they had gone well. Something kept telling me to rank my choices based more on how *I felt* at the interview, and I have already talked about the importance of trusting gut instinct.

When I interviewed with the University of Florida—which had a well-respected hand program—my interview began like all the others. I readied myself by dressing in my best, donning a smart pair of four-inch heels and my pearls. By this time in my life, I always interviewed in heels and pearls; it satisfied both my sense of style and my family's tradition of dressing to distinguish ourselves. Pearls always made me feel elegant and confident.

The first half of the interview was fairly standard, and I got a good vibe from the fellows and attendings there. When the meeting felt like it was concluding, I was a little surprised—it wasn't nearly as long as the other interviews thus far. As my interviewer rose from her seat, I stood too, preparing to tell her how much I appreciated her time.

But before I could speak, she smiled and said, "Okay, if you'll follow me, I'll take you back to the OR and we can get you into some scrubs. Then I'll introduce you to Dr. Paul Dell, who will take over from there."

Since this was before the time of masks, I hid the surprise from my face. As you've no doubt already guessed, I had no idea that part of the interview would be conducted in the operating room! I managed to smile and nod, however, and she showed me where I was headed next.

Then, the woman handed me a set of scrubs. "Go ahead and change here," she said, indicating a dressing room. "Come on out when you're done."

I went into the room, put on the scrubs, and took off my heels. Of course I left my pearls on. Looking at my heels for a lingering moment, I finally slid my feet back into them. Those lovely sky-high heels were the only shoes I had, and they were completely unsuited to the task.

You can do this, Lattisha. Play through the pain.

And it did become painful, I can tell you. Heels like that aren't meant to be worn while constantly walking and standing. Still, even this part of the interview seemed to be going well. I instantly liked Dr. Dell, and we had an easy back-and-forth flow as I answered his questions and I asked mine.

Unfortunately, as time went on, the pain in my feet grew more and more excruciating. At one point, while Dr. Dell was talking and I was trying to listen, I kept shifting my weight from foot to foot, toe to heel, trying to find a more comfortable way to stand and walk. I was beginning to worry that my feet were already bleeding.

Then I realized Dr. Dell had gone silent and was looking at me expectantly. *Oh, my God, he asked me something.* Instead of asking him to repeat himself, I blurted out, "I'm so sorry, but would it be possible for me to use the restroom?"

Once I got into the bathroom, I sat down and finally, finally removed those torture devices from my poor feet. No blood yet, thankfully. But what was I going to do?

I couldn't answer more questions or try to do any procedures in those heels; the thought of putting them back on made me want to weep. I wasn't even wearing panty hose—Gainesville, Florida, was just too hot for that—so I was completely barefoot.

Then I looked at the shoe covers I had taken off with the heels.

Could I do that? Should I do that?

I thought about the vibe I had gotten from the interview so far, and I thought, *You know what? They like you already. And you like them. So leave the freaking heels off, Lattisha. Put on those shoe covers, get back out there, and kill this interview.*

So I did. I finished that interview with no shoes, and they never knew the difference, as far as I could tell. I left the facility with those heels back on my aching feet, walking gingerly back to my car, with the distinct feeling that I had found my number-one rank.

LESSON

When your back is against the wall, sometimes it's best to innovate and push through.

HEELS AND PEARLS

Much the same way that I had once rejected the advice of interviewing for General Surgery residency as a plan B to Orthopaedic Surgery residency, I never really accepted the idea of ranking my top fellowship choices based on their prestige. The clout I might earn from being able to say I was a fellow at Such-and-Such University's hand program wasn't a priority for me; what I wanted was to learn as much as possible from excellent surgeons in a supportive work environment. My residency had been five years of grueling work in a variety of pressure-filled environments, and I was now looking for a place to sharpen my skill set.

My gut was telling me that the University of Florida's hand program would be a good experience, so when the time came, I ranked them as my top choice. I was delighted to find that I matched with them. My instincts about the program were proven right when upon my acceptance, I discovered I had been *their* top choice for that year's cohort, as well.

On my first day in the program, when I got the chance to greet Dr. Dell again, he said, "What—no heels today?"

"Um, no," I laughed. Apparently, I'd made a bigger impression on Dr. Dell than I thought.

"I'm a little disappointed," he joked. "I remembered those heels, click-click-clicking behind me as you followed me from room to room."

"I don't usually wear heels when I'm operating," I replied, confidently. "But I do wear them to the clinic, and I always operate in pearls."

"Hey, you can own it. That's one of the reasons I chose you out of all those other applicants." He grinned at me. "No one, male or female, would have had the audacity to wear heels in the operating room."

When I laughed, that clinched our budding friendship, and just like that, my fellowship year was off to a promising start.

Dr. Dell took me under his wing, and I found myself working with a new mentor at the top of his game personally and professionally; he earned my boundless respect right away. One of the attributes I loved about his mentoring style was that he always treated me with respect—not as a student or mentee, but as a less-experienced peer—and that made all the difference.

Despite our instant rapport, however, I couldn't let myself perform less than my best. Dr. Dell may have liked my heels and pearls, but I still had to show him why I was worthy to be his top choice for that fellowship.

LESSON

Stay confident and own your style.

My First Validation

While I had found my comfort zone in terms of work environment and colleagues, *comfortable* didn't mean *easy*. I hadn't spent much time focusing on hand surgery during my residency, so I found myself dealing with yet another steep learning curve.

Those first few months of fellowship went by in a blur—I worked my ass off, and as a result, I was exhausted most of the time. I knew I was in the right place, however, not just because of how much I was learning, but because of Dr. Dell's guidance and expertise.

I watched every move he made, absorbing his techniques, from how he moved his tenotomy scissors to how he dressed the patient. This was my first chance to really immerse myself in the art of hand surgery, and I loved it, especially being in the operating room.

A few months into my fellowship, I was performing a procedure while Dr. Dell sat across from me. Suddenly, he said, "You know, you are *really* good."

That pronouncement, so calm and certain, floored me, but I tried to laugh it off. "What? It's a pretty basic procedure," I said, tucking my head.

"No," he said, once again stating it like a fact—something I should already know. "I've watched you in the operating room. You're an excellent surgeon."

I'm not generally a crier, and that's a good thing, because I would have been a mess just then. As it was, those words threatened to make me melt into the floor with happiness. I finished that procedure feeling like I could conquer the world—or at least, fix all its hand and forearm pain.

Up until my fellowship, I'd been told *no* and been made to feel unworthy of my progress toward my dream for far too long. This was the first time someone in a position of authority genuinely and openly applauded me for my work as a doctor. I felt seen as an orthopaedic surgeon who was applying her skills and honing her craft—and not only was I seen by someone in a higher position than my own, but someone renowned in the field.

Dr. Dell was (and still is) the number-one hand surgeon in the State of Florida. He was well-known on a national level; the people in my residency had heard of him and knew his reputation. At that point in his career, he'd trained over sixty hand surgeons.

Dr. Dell telling me I was an excellent surgeon was like winning an Oscar, a Grammy, and the Super Bowl all at once. Internally, I had told myself I was a worthy fellow to be trained. Dr. Dell's validation helped to secure the internal monologue, however, and silenced any seeds of self-doubt that tried to take root.

Hey Morehouse!

During my fellowship year working with Dr. Dell, I was often the first Black woman in many of our work environments. To some extent, this was because I was the first Black woman Dr. Dell had ever brought on board as a fellow.

One day, Dr. Dell and I staffed a small clinic where there were no residents, so we were the only two surgeons. When I enter new hospital environments, it's typical that at some point, people question where I went to undergraduate, medical school, and so forth. It was during one of these conversations that I told a White male nurse that I attended Morehouse School of Medicine, a historically Black medical school. Despite me introducing myself as Dr. Bilbrew, from that point on, that nurse addressed me as *Hey, Morehouse*, or *Sure, Morehouse*, while he always addressed Dr. Dell as *Dr. Dell.*

I just took it in stride as one of those minor interactions that I didn't necessarily see as offensive. After all, I had been called worse, and I knew most of the staff in these smaller clinics weren't used to seeing a Black woman as a surgeon. No harm, no foul.

Dr. Dell didn't see it this way, however. When he heard the nurse address me as *Morehouse*, Dr. Dell rounded on the man with a scowl. "Call her Dr. Bilbrew, damn it. That's her name," he snapped. "She's my fellow and a board-eligible orthopaedic surgeon."

The nurse's eyes went wide. "I didn't mean anything by it, sir—"

"You've never once called any of my other fellows by the city they're from, or their college name," Dr. Dell said coldly. "To you and everyone else in this clinic, she is Dr. Bilbrew. I never want to hear otherwise again."

I was speechless; it really hadn't occurred to me to find the nickname offensive. When the nurse turned to me and said, "I'm sorry, Dr. Bilbrew. It won't happen again," I could only nod and murmur something akin to, "That's okay."

I didn't get a chance to talk to Dr. Dell about this incident until we were on our way home, but even then, I couldn't find the words to begin the conversation. Finally, Dr. Dell broached the topic. "I'm sorry about what happened there," he said.

I thought he was apologizing for making a scene. "It's okay," I began.

"No, it really isn't." He sighed, looking grim. "You get treated differently, and that's *not* okay."

I have talked before about how Dr. Dell was the first experienced medical professional to treat me as if we were on the same level; that day, he was the first person with authority to openly and loudly speak out on my behalf. Throughout my fellowship and beyond, Dr. Dell demonstrated again and again that he was an advocate for me the same way I wanted to become my Nanny's advocate as a physician.

Now that I'm a shareholder in my own practice, I try to channel Dr. Dell's sponsorship and advocacy into how I treat both my mentees and my patients. When someone in authority treats you based on who you are as a human being, it shows you what the world can and should be—and it makes you want to provide other people with the same consideration.

I also see Dr. Dell and his sponsorship as a shining example of how to continue striving for success and to adapt to new challenges. If I stop trying to improve myself and rest on my laurels, I am going to go stagnant. I'm going to lose the fuel for new achievements and new adventures, and risk losing the status and position that will allow me more traction to pull others like me up to my level, and even beyond it.

This is why, despite having successfully reached my goal of becoming an orthopaedic surgeon and a shareholder in my company, I don't consider myself to have truly *made it*. There's still just too much to do.

LESSON

Aim for the moon, and *if* you don't make it, you'll land amongst the stars.

THE ART OF THE BALANCE

It didn't take long for me to regard Dr. Dell as more than a mentor; he was actually a sponsor. A sponsor doesn't simply show you the ropes and provide advice and feedback; they provide opportunities for you to be successful and place you center-stage to maximize those opportunities. They advocate for your advancement in every way, including supporting the risks you take and ensuring that you find a good balance between the personal and professional.

During my time working with Dr. Dell, I learned a great deal about the science of being a hand surgeon. So many of the techniques I employ today in the OR are skills I either learned from him, or perfected under his tutelage.

The process of learning to be a surgeon is an individual journey, however, so he also taught me to balance the science of surgery with the art of making it my own. Dr. Dell encouraged me to develop my own style more fully and trust myself to lean into my strengths, regardless of how others do things.

Dr. Dell also taught me the importance of giving back. Being a good surgeon meant more than what you could offer your patients in the OR; it also involved how you could give to your community outside of the OR. Once again, he did this by example: he and his wife, Ruthie, founded a camp for children with congenital upper-limb differences called Hands to Love. Every year, they host a three-day Hand Camp, and the organization itself is a year-round hub for a nationwide support network for these kids, their parents, and their caregivers.

There's a balance to learn here: how to apply the science of orthopaedic surgery and the art of helping others in a way that benefits not only their bodies, but their hearts and minds also.

Like any truly great sponsor, Dr. Dell wanted me to not only succeed but *thrive* in the profession we shared. To that end, he would say that you have to make space for those who need you—and by that, he meant family and friends.

Dr. Dell taught me the art of balance between my work life and my personal life. Like him, I enjoy life and make the most of my free time, whether that means spending time with my family, making time to read a book, or relaxing with a glass of good wine.

He was also a major proponent for traveling. Dr. Dell worked hard, but he also took vacations every few months to travel with his wife and get away from the operating room. I never knew anyone who traveled so extensively. Any time I sent an email or placed a call to him, I never knew where I would find him—he would respond, "I'm in Panama!" or "I'm in the south of France!" or "I'm in New York!" The journey was something he delighted in and reinforced in me to continue. Traveling, even as a busy medical professional, clears the mind while simultaneously filling it with new experiences, cultures, and adventures.

Once, I asked him, "So, you've been traveling like this your whole career?"

He nodded. "Literally the entire time I've been practicing. I mean, you have to."

Then he gave me a look that was pure *Oh, Lattisha*. "You have to have balance," he explained. "You have to spend time with your family. You have to appreciate your friends. If you don't," he shook his head and chuckled, "you'll lose your marbles."

Even when we were working, he would find a way to make our time together enjoyable. He and I often drove together to surgeries and clinics, and after exhausting days of sometimes seeing what felt like one hundred patients, he would insist that we find a new restaurant to try. Or maybe he wanted to take me to a Greek restaurant he'd been going to for years, or maybe hang out with some of his old friends in the area. We always took time to relax, reflect, and enjoy life.

Dr. Dell showed me that it was possible to balance working hard with having a life, and for that, I am immeasurably grateful. It's because of him that I have the tools to keep myself from getting burned out—a real danger for someone in our line of work.

Whenever I need proof that balance is the key, I look at Dr. Dell's career. Thanks to him, I know finding and maintaining that balance can be difficult, but that balance is the key to keeping your marbles. Dr. Dell is in his seventies and still practicing, but more importantly, still teaching; I hope to one day say the same about myself. And it will never feel like a burden, but a gift.

PHYSICIAN, LOVE (AND TRUST) THYSELF

Without Dr. Dell, I might never have understood the beauty of loving the art of what you do above the practicality of your skill set. This way of thinking about surgery helps me to avoid burnout and maintain a healthy work–life balance. I will never cease to be grateful for my time with him; I wouldn't be half the surgeon I am today without his guidance.

And I might never have met Dr. Dell, much less benefitted from his wisdom, surgical skill, or friendship, if I had ranked my fellowship options the way everyone told me to.

If I had ranked one of those other programs higher simply because of prestige, I guarantee my experience would not have been the same. I wouldn't have had a wonderful year of working in a supportive partnership while learning the art and science of hand surgery. My time at the University of Florida set the foundation for me to become the hand surgeon I am today.

When it came to this particular choice, it simply didn't make sense for me to categorize or prioritize my options based on the opinions of others. While you should always seek wisdom when you're making a major decision, you also have to know yourself well enough to understand what is best for you. Sometimes that will track with what everyone else is telling you to do, but sometimes it won't; you have to be ready to pivot onto the path that makes the most sense for you.

This requires a significant amount of self-confidence and internal reflection—but those are tools, just like everything else. You can learn them and improve your use of them with practice.

Being adaptable along the way will help. Use what you have at your disposal and discard anything that gets in your way. Take a page from Lattisha's Book of Interview Near-Calamities: If the only shoes you have to wear are going to make you less effective, kick 'em off and go barefoot. And if people see you this way or comment on it, own your actions. Be confident in those choices.

And I highly recommend finding a mentor who can be a sponsor, someone you can learn from, who will always have your back, and go down swinging to protect it.

Now, as a mentor myself, I look back at the examples that have been set for me by my grandparents, my parents, and my own mentors. Because of them and what they've done for me, I know there's another group of people I have to leave space for: those who are coming up behind me and potentially following in my footsteps.

Like my parents, I may have built in silence for much of my training, but I always wanted the trail I blazed to make things easier for the next Lattisha. I don't want women—particularly those who look like me, or medical students who came late to orthopaedics like I did—to struggle just because I had to struggle. I will never be that person, watching dispassionately as the baby bird flies or falls on their first trip out of the nest. Instead, I want those future Lattishas to know this path is worth every ounce of their struggle.

I want to be an example of someone who has struggled but succeeded, someone who has a healthy, balanced life and career—and I want my example to be a beacon to others who want to achieve the same kind of goals. This especially extends to other women of color. There may be power in being the only one in the room, but

I want to see more women like me doing this job and enjoying it the way I do.

So remember: everything we do reflects who we are, whether we are the mentee or the mentor. Along the way, you have to stick to your standards of excellence and how others should be treated. Your consistent and effective efforts will lead to the feeling of professional fulfillment when someone with more experience respects your contributions and treats you like a peer.

Thanks to Dr. Dell and his unwavering sponsorship, I make a point to treat all my students and mentees with respect as people and as future physicians; I never forget that they will soon be my peers, just as I'm now Dr. Dell's—wild as that still sounds to me.

9

THE FIRST FIVE YEARS

After years of supervision and scrutiny in the operating room during my residency and fellowship, stepping into my career as an orthopaedic surgeon brought with it a new sense of freedom—and even more responsibility.

Now, when I walk into an operating room to perform a procedure, I'm usually the only surgeon there, and there's both power and privilege in that kind of leadership position. While some surgeons enjoy this power and privilege to the point their egos swell into god complexes, I believe most can and do retain a certain amount of humility.

When you're the one in the room with the most authority, you're also the one with the most responsibility toward the patient's health and safety. Everyone from the patient to the anesthesiologist to the nurse to the scrub tech is looking to you for information and direction from the moment you arrive—and you can find yourself and your abilities put to the test in a split-second. Despite you being the head of a team, that room is pointless without you in it—for better, or for worse.

Early in my practice, I performed a surgery on a patient who had a mass on her forearm; it had been growing there for some time. While I closed up the patient, I hummed a bit, reflecting on the details of the procedure—it had been fairly routine with no complications. *Nothing wrong with that,* I thought contentedly. Every successful surgery was a great one in my book. Once the patient was bandaged and everything looked as it should, I deflated the tourniquet and prepared to scrub out, and that's when things went sideways.

Right before my eyes, patches of red began oozing through layers of gauze and bandage on the patient's arm. *Whoa.* There's often a bit of bleeding when the blood begins flowing back into the arm after we remove the tourniquet, but this was an unusual amount.

I opened my mouth to say something to the nurse, but before I could speak, the ooze became a cascade of pulsating blood pouring out from the bandages. At the same moment, the monitors sounded an alarm as the patient's blood pressure plummeted. *Oh, God—that's a major artery.*

There was no one else in the room, no chief resident or attending, to appeal to for help. I was the surgeon—and I was the only one in the room who could fix the problem, with the help of my team.

In a split-second, I stood beside the patient, undoing the bandages and putting the tourniquet back on, talking to the people in the room with every bit of calm I could muster. "All right, let the tourniquet back up. We're opening the patient again," I said. "We need to find the source of bleeding. Get the hemostats ready." And we got to work.

It was not a time for panic or for shouting; neither of those would have helped anyone in that room. The best thing I could do for my patient and my team was to stay cool in those endless minutes of working to save the patient from crashing.

Things went right, and then things went wrong, but I just kept breathing and working. The poor scrub tech in the OR was a student who had never seen anything like what was happening —it was a frightening amount of blood—so when he inevitably couldn't keep up, I simply told him, "I need you to scrub out and get your teacher," without missing a beat. We stabilized the patient, who postoperatively showed no adverse effects, and she went on to be newly diagnosed with a vascular disease that likely contributed to her nearly bleeding out that day.

This was one of those life-or-death moments in the OR, and I'm proud to say I rose to that challenge—in that moment, when my patient's life was on the line, I fully owned being a surgeon. Sometimes it takes something as drastic as a crashing patient to fully grasp the power and privilege you have as the leader of the OR team.

LESSON

When placed in a position of leadership, draw from your skill set...but also lean heavily on humility, conciseness of thought, and a calm but direct disposition.

POWER AND PRIVILEGE

Stepping into a place of power and privilege can be more intimidating for anyone who isn't a White cishet man. The glass ceiling is a tricky kind of obstacle—one that is sometimes present psychologically and systemically. Society has dictated for so long that in a room full of people, the leader is less likely a woman or minority.

As a Black woman, I have felt that pressure to represent not only myself but also my race and my gender when in the operating room. I have to remind myself to be comfortable in a leadership position when, much of the time, the members of my team in the room don't look like me or are much older than me.

When you have spent so much of your life and your career battling through barriers and dealing with disrespect, you can get burned out. I once heard an older Black female physician remark that her journey in medicine dealing with constant microaggressions felt like death by a thousand cuts; in other words, you can exhaust yourself emotionally and physically with frustration when it feels like nothing's changing, despite your efforts. You might begin to wonder, *What is the point of all this?*

I would love to work with ten other people who look like me, but the truth is I'm sometimes the first Black woman orthopaedic surgeon to work with other healthcare providers, and I'm the first Black female orthopaedic surgeon to operate at some medical facilities. I can't have a chip on my shoulder about that.

LESSON

Change the lens through which you view the environment. It's no longer a lens of difficulty or burden; it's a lens of preparation and ability: *I'm here, I'm ready, and I trained for this.*

I can't look around the operating room and ask, *Why am I the only Black woman in this room?* Instead, I have to flip that to a power statement: I have to look around the operating room and say, *I am the only Black woman in this room.* I have to step up to the plate, accept the power I have earned and the privilege of my leadership position, and most importantly, successfully beast this surgical pathology in front of me.

Breaking that barrier means I am an example for everyone who sees me in my role as an orthopaedic surgeon. When I represent well, those people may never again look at a Black woman like *she can't handle the operating room* or *she doesn't belong here*. Instead, it might permeate their subconscious mind: *Black women can be surgeons*, because they saw Dr. Bilbrew do it.

It's true that I have often had to struggle with earning respect from those in the surgical and hospital setting when so many other surgeons don't; it is tiring to constantly have to assert who I am and that I have earned my right to stand in the operating room. It also keeps me grounded, motivated, and humbled, however, to continue striving to clear the path for those who follow me.

Some surgeons seem to love the idea of power even more than their jobs—and definitely more than their team. I have worked with surgeons who are arrogant jackasses in the OR, striding into the room as if it's an absolute monarchy and they are the king while the other members of the team are mere peasants. Unfortunately, no one has reminded these people that being skilled within your surgical specialty doesn't give you the right to treat everyone else as beneath you or lesser-than, since all have very specific roles that contribute to the surgery's success.

Then, there are surgeons whose disillusioned self-importance tends to be less focused on the team effort and more focused on how the patient should be grateful to the surgeon for deigning to perform their procedure. *This patient is lucky I'm here. They should be happy I'm even treating them.* There's also more marked lack of accountability from these surgeons, with more blame for the patient than acceptance of responsibility when problems arise.

I have worked hard to avoid these two extremes while still finding a comfortable balance with my power and privilege; even now, however, I still caution myself to maintain appropriate pride in myself and what I can do. After years of dealing with the annoyance of being doubted for my potential and going unrecognized for my skills, now when I step onto the stage of the operating room, I have the same confidence and humility my five-year-old self had when I first declared I would enter medicine to protect patients like my Nanny.

FRONT AND CENTER STAGE

During my residency, I remember an attending who told me, "You know, it takes about five years before you're really comfortable in your practice."

What a load of crap, I thought at the time, rather smugly. *Who's got five years to get comfortable in this job?*

Well, as it turns out…me. As of this writing, I am in my sixth year of practice, and I have learned that attending was absolutely right. While it did not take five years to learn how to perform a simple trigger-finger release, I have thoughtfully and delicately refined, honed, and dissected every skill I was given. It *has* taken me every bit of these five years to learn what it means to be a practicing surgeon, and to develop the tools I need to function expediently and efficiently in this role, in terms of surgical *and* psychological skills. The foundation was set for me as far back as my grandparents coming to England; during my path to success, their foundation was built upon and strengthened by my allies, mentors, and sponsors. Now that I have made it this far, however, it's up to me to demonstrate why I deserve to be not only a part of the surgical team but the head of it.

Being a resident and then a fellow is a little like spending six years in the chorus of a dance company or as a supporting player in a theater troupe. You're present, you're visible, you're a member of the team, but you are not in a lead role. Then you start your first year of surgical practice, and it's showtime once again—only this time, you are the star, positioned center-stage every day, wielding the power and privilege that come with it.

It can be difficult to keep perspective in that kind of situation and not let yourself become a diva, the kind of surgeon everyone hates to work with. To that end, I use three specific filters to keep myself balanced.

First and foremost, you have to remember you are a leader, so everything has to be filtered through the lens of accountability. Accept that responsibility, and own it. When you start to take on that leadership filter, it affects how you interact with people too, so the next two filters are just as important.

Just as important is the filter of kindness. Within the surgical world, it is difficult for someone, especially a woman, to maintain a culture of kindness without having their kindness mistaken for weakness; however, if you don't approach others with kindness, you run the risk of forgetting who you are and where you came from. The ability to wield kindness in the face of adversity is both powerful and a privilege. As a leader, you have to learn how to balance kindness with authority—the goal here is not to be everyone's best friend but to stay humble in your dealings with your team. When necessary, you can dial back the kindness and dial up the authority to find your voice and be a leader for your team.

The last of the three filters is humility. As much as the surgical process starts and ends with you, there's an excellent chance you won't be the most experienced and knowledgeable person in the room in certain situations. You may be the most important person in the room, but you don't know everything just because you have earned a medical degree. Many times, the best thing you can do for your patient is listen when someone else speaks up and says, "I've seen this before; let me help you."

Just like everything else, using these filters as tools takes practice, and you'll make mistakes along the way. Some will be more mortifying than others, and those encounters can create the most memorable lessons.

For example, during my first year of practice, I was at a new-to-me hospital prepping for a procedure, and I was ready to begin the surgery when the scrub tech told me, "No, we shouldn't drape the patient yet."

"No," I said, struggling to keep my patience. It had already been a long day. "We've got them scrubbed down and ready, so we're going to drape and start."

"No, we're not," she insisted. "We need to wait two minutes."

My temper flared. *Who does this scrub tech think she is?* "You know what? Why don't you scrub out, and go get me someone else who'll actually work with me." Never mind that this would have taken far longer than two minutes—Dr. Bilbrew had lost some patience, along with her temper.

To her credit, the scrub tech stood her ground. "No problem, if you don't want to work with me," she said evenly. "But it's a new hospital rule that we have to wait for this prep fluid to dry for two minutes. A patient was burned when we started the procedure without letting it dry thoroughly."

Oh, damn. I was up on my high horse, looking down and feeling a little nauseated as I realized just how far I had gotten from solid ground. I'd thrown both my humility and kindness filters out the window, only to find out I was completely in the wrong.

I did the only thing I could do—the only thing the leadership filter would allow me to do: I took responsibility for my actions. "My apologies. I was 100 percent out of line," I told her. "There is no excuse for not listening to you when you were following hospital mandates and patient safety. I don't want you to scrub out. Please stay, if you are comfortable working with me."

Thankfully, she stayed, and after the operation, we had a good talk about the situation and about different safety checks. And any time I'm tempted to look past my humility filter and get all puffed up with my own importance, I think about this experience and check my actions before I make an misinformed decision or statement.

CHECK YOURSELF BEFORE YOU WRECK YOURSELF

Being the only one in the room who looks like you can become exhausting—and more than that, it can be lonely. But don't quit. We need our medical workplace to reflect the world around us, because when it doesn't, there is too much inequality and imbalance of power.

Being a leader from that position means you can impact more than just the people around you; you're directly influencing the people coming up behind you. Blaze that trail for them, and you'll be actively working to make the world more equitable for all—even when that means more pain for you as the one who cleared the path.

The three filters—accountability, kindness, humility—are crucial to maintaining emotional and mental health while balancing the power and privilege of your position. Like all tools, they require practice, and like many other types of filters, sometimes you have to layer them to ensure you're performing at your best. Remember, the spotlight is on you.

Unfortunately, being in the spotlight can also make you an easy and attractive target.

10

SCALPEL, STAT

Recently, I read an article in an orthopaedic journal that stated the medical staff who are most likely to be second-guessed by members of their team are minorities and women. I have certainly been the target of doubt, second-guessing, and other forms of negativity during my years of practice, and some of it felt like sabotage—like the person who should have been supporting me as team leader was actively working against me from the inside.

During my first five years of practice, I worked with plenty of people who said things like, *We're here to support you, Dr. Bilbrew,* but their actions clearly communicated the opposite. I have learned to pay closer attention to what people do rather than what they say; that's the only way you can determine who is truly on your side and working with you for the benefit of the team and the patient.

Most of the time, practicing medicine is not a one-person show; it's a team effort. Surgery, especially, requires a team that functions as a cohesive unit. So when there are complications and discrepancies within the team, it's going to be up to you to solve them—even when the problem in question involves another team member's issues with you. It can be a tiring job that requires you to find your voice in uncomfortable situations. As cliché as it sounds, your modus operandi needs to follow the advice of that well-known Bob Marley song: *"Get up, stand up, stand up for your rights / Get up, stand up, don't give up the fight!"*

Recently, I worked with a competent nurse who, whenever she interacted with me, always seemed to quickly become incompetent and lackadaisical. She demonstrated time and again that she didn't respect me or my needs as the surgeon, despite paying me polite lip service, especially in front of others.

Our interactions had been increasingly frustrating for me, but the most recent one involved prepping my pre-operative patient's chart for surgery, which somehow, she never had prepared—despite that being one of her duties for assisting me. I asked her for the chart, only for her to tell me it was *somewhere* and she was sure *someone* had it.

This vagueness was the straw that broke Dr. Bilbrew's kindness filter. Now was the time to get up and stand up.

"Who is *someone*, and where are they located?" I asked, trying not to let my tone get too volatile. "Because *someone* seems to have *my* chart every time I need it." She demurred, all innocent, but we had reached our tipping point. The only way to truly deal with something like this is to actually discuss it face-to-face at the time.

LESSON

You will encounter many battles on your journey; choose which ones you'll engage, and do so wisely. Be prepared, be calm, and be ready to execute.

"Listen," I said. "For the last four years, whenever I ask you for help, you tend to put it off on someone else or slide away from the responsibility. How can we come up with a plan that doesn't give you extra work, but also provides me with what I need to do my job properly?" I asked. "What do you think would be the best way to do that?"

And just like that, we were having a dialogue. It wasn't comfortable, but it worked, and we came up with a plan she followed from that point on. That nurse and I never did become friendly, but we worked together much better after our conversation. She realized I wasn't going to allow her to actively undermine me any longer. By asking for her input instead of demanding the respect she had not been giving me, I corrected it using a positive and demonstrative approach.

There will be people on your team who should be helping you, but they very obviously aren't—either they undermine your authority, or they underperform the tasks you ask them to perform, or they attack who you are as a leader. Sometimes these people will be subtle, but often they won't; it will be up to you to both learn to recognize them and to learn how to deal with them. How can you tell the people bent on sabotage from the ones who are providing genuine and useful dissent?

LESSON

When dealing with conflict, especially when you are the lead, speak slowly, maintain eye contact, and be deliberate with your words.

Generally, they will show themselves through their actions, which will often be very different from their words; it will be on you to keep your eyes open for this kind of duality. Airing the problem is a great start, but you also have to initiate a solution as part of the discussion. You are a leader, so you aren't just playing the blame game; you're trying to improve the team, and unless you're experiencing serious harassment or actual sabotage, you're not trying to get anyone fired. Unless they commit a serious offense, you're going to have to work with these people in the future. The best thing you can do—both for your patients and your peace of mind—is rehabilitate them and set the expectations and standards of what they should bring to their interactions with you. Just remember, life is hard; there's no point in making it harder for anyone else, or allowing anyone else to make it harder for you.

KNIVES OUT

When you lead from the front, as I always try to do, you unavoidably leave yourself open to potential backstabbing—and the world is often an unfriendly place for minorities and women in positions of leadership. Orthopaedic surgery is a White, male-dominated medical field, which is not always inclusive and inviting. Yet it is in these scenarios of uncomfortability and exclusion that women and people of color can have the greatest impact once they enter the room. Though you may get fatigued by the constant barrage and unsupportive environment in which you may work or train, you must persevere. You persevere for your family, for your future, for your patients, and for those who will follow behind you.

Yes, it can be difficult to maintain a culture of kindness, reciprocity, and respect when you feel like you must constantly validate your presence in the room. You have power and privilege, but you also have to deal with team members who may doubt you or actively look for ways to disrespect you. It can be a full-time job to constantly place the mental energy to keep from becoming bitter and hardened by this kind of environment if you don't have the support you need. Going into an operating room with a *you better damned well respect me!* attitude, however, will detract from your effectiveness as a team leader and a surgeon... and can even be a detriment to patient safety.

If you are able to maintain that filter of kindness, humility, and accountability—using your own experiences as someone who's been excluded for the majority of your life already—you can make your teammates and co-workers feel needed and appreciated, thereby cultivating a culture of respect, equality, and inclusiveness. This perspective can make your work life better in many ways, not the least of which by ensuring you don't push away the people who are truly there to support you while deflecting those who might mean you harm. Overall, this approach improves the surgical team, which means better patient care.

But what about those situations in which you're being openly disrespected or you have hard, unmistakable evidence of sabotage?

One of my favorite phrases about dealing with obstacles is this: *you can't cut out the negative using a butter knife.* There are times when you have to sharply and intently remove malignancy from your life, and that is where kindness and gentleness has no place or purpose. Some situations require a scalpel or a razor to make sure you cut quickly and cleanly—which means standing up for yourself with bluntness and intensity, in the moment, if possible.

As an example, take the nurse with a grudge: if she hadn't followed the plan we agreed upon—and that I documented in my follow-up email—then I would have had an actionable reason to bring in her supervisor. I've had to do that a few times during my practice, unfortunately, but getting out the saboteurs makes the team stronger. (There's an "bad-apple" metaphor I could use here, but you get the point.) Cut out the malignant cancer, before it causes systemic organ failure. The cancer is the insubordinate teammate, the organ failure is the team that collapses when that teammate is allowed to roam recklessly without consequence.

I have been able to keep myself both vigilant in terms of watching for sabotage and able to maintain my filter of kindness. I never forget that I have to foster a positive environment for my team, but I don't try to be everyone's friend. While I rarely have to openly demand respect from those I work with, I do make sure that, if personal grudges or issues come into the picture, I project one simple rule: *You don't have to like me, but if you're in my OR, you* do *have to work cohesively with me.* And I can confidently report that most team members thoroughly enjoy working in my operating room.

When it comes down to it, there are very few people in my professional orbit who are on my *People I Cannot Work With* list, and based on the methodology I employ toward my team, I also feel confident I'm not on many of those lists.

I've had to exchange my butter knife for a scalpel more than once, and each instance made those environments a better place. I even made friends out of former detractors, although more often, the working relationship was simply severed in one form or another. It's all about balance and timing—knowing when kindness and patience are no longer beneficial and must be replaced with sternness and sharpness of mind and tongue. In situations such as these, it is important that you find the strength of your own voice.

Any time I end up in conflict with someone in a professional setting, I have to make my case with caution. I have literally practiced making my case out loud in order to say everything the best way possible. My father taught me to deepen my voice to give it more impact, because there can be no whine or cracks in your voice when you speak up to defend yourself. I do my best to keep passion in my heart and objectivity in my voice.

Women are often given this kind of advice for self-advocating, because high-pitched voices and anything that sounds *whiny* often gets us stigmatized as irrational and overly emotional. Black women, especially, have to be careful. I know I personally always have a voice in the back of my head preaching caution: *You don't want to be the angry Black woman. You want them to hire other Black women someday.* Though this is by no means fair to who I am as a person and who I represent as a Black woman, perception is, unfortunately, reality until you rise to a position to prove it otherwise and break down those ill-conceived perceptions.

Certain people in authority *want* someone like me to be the Angry Black Woman, because that makes it easier for them to adhere to their perception. They want to be able to say, *She was abrasive and difficult to deal with,* so they can label me as the problem. So even when I have the right to be all of that, I can't give in, because it will reinforce the stereotype and give them more ammunition. Staying calm and speaking with a modulated tone, even when you're seething inside, is an important tool when you're trying to be heard.

LESSON

When in a heated discussion with someone who gaslights your anger, reply calmly and decisively: "Do not confuse my tone for my objectivity and passion for truth, and definitely not for the position I've earned to state it."

DISSECT *CRITICS* FROM *CRITIQUES*

When we work with the public, we never work in a vacuum. We are always being evaluated while we work—by those we work with, and by those whom we serve. For that reason, criticism is an ever-present factor. Critiques are invaluable as you train for your career, but you should not try to please people who offer judgmental, subjective criticism, for a variety of reasons.

The first time I remember being subject to major criticism was back in Handsworth as my parents were preparing to move us to America. We were second-generation members of a tight-knit community there, socially and through our church, so perhaps that's why people there reacted so strongly when word got around about my parents' plan. More or less, the entire community came out as critical of my parents' decision, disputing how the move was ill-fated and would ruin my sister and me. As young as I was at the time, I was fairly insulated from the motivation and meaning behind our community's disapproval, but I still felt the sting.

In the end, of course, my parents ignored their critics and pushed through with their plans, regardless of what other people thought. As an adult, I understand now that those people in Handsworth had no idea of how hard my parents were working to make the move successful; they didn't know how much time went into the decision or how much research my parents had done. They simply saw what to them would be a terrifying prospect—moving to a brand-new, intimidating country—and reacted with criticism founded only in their own preconceived notions.

To me, this is a perfect example of how to delineate between *criticism* and *critique*. Critiques are offered by someone who is qualified to give you objective, actionable feedback, and ideally, this should be someone who not only knows more than you about what you're trying to accomplish but also knows the context for your actions. Criticism, on the other hand, is often subjective or personal, delivered by people who are ignorant of those elements of the situation. The problem? Sometimes, criticism and critique can look and sound very much alike.

If you are trying to determine whether or not to listen to one of your critics, look at their qualifications and level of understanding first. Consider the source, and if their bona fides check out, then consider their words.

If your critic is qualified to offer feedback, consider their motivations when it comes to you, personally. Are they critiquing you to support you or to antagonize you? There is a big difference there, and while sometimes their words or tone will indicate their true motivations, you may also need to look at their past and present actions.

Anyone offering you a true critique meant to help you will not only deliver objective guidance from a qualified perspective but will also work with you to create an action plan that will help you succeed. Ideally, they will do this with kindness and consideration. Criticism has its roots in making sure you never reach your goal, but critique helps you reach the next level in your journey.

While listening to critiques will become a major part of achieving your goal while you're in training, listening to criticism will do the opposite. If my parents had let the people of Handsworth influence their decisions, we would never have left—and while I'd like to think otherwise, there would have been a good chance I would never have become an orthopaedic surgeon.

You have to trust in those who have an eye toward your success, not those who would tear you down while you're reaching up on your climb to the top.

Practice Makes Progress

There's a reason we refer to medicine as "practice"—it's a continual and ever-changing environment requiring constant vigilance. I have spent my first five years honing my practical skills through ongoing training and practice and learning new and better tools, mentally and physically. The tools I use to deal with the people on my team are among the most important, and I use and adapt them every day.

Among those tools:

- → **Be calm, be humble, and listen.** I have learned the most from this one, as I've already discussed.
- → **Process in stages.** Don't react until you have processed something from multiple angles; even if you need a quick response, take a few seconds to consider your words before you speak.
- → **Stand firm.** If all the evidence tells you that you are right, don't waver.
- → **Document and detail everything.** Write down any and all incidents involving interactions with others, because you never know when you might need that information.
- → **Be strategic.** Every interaction is a chance to make an impact.
- → **Choose your team wisely.** The foundation of your first few years depends on who is there to assist you as you grow.

- **Be available and be agreeable.** You will have to create your own air of positivity around your work.
- **Carry your cards.** Your professional information could be useful at the oddest times, so always have a few business cards with you.
- **Be a teacher.** Being open and willing to answer questions will not only help those in training and working with you, but it will also keep you on your toes.
- **Don't be afraid to accept a challenge . . . but don't be afraid to turn one down, either.** This may feel like a contradiction in terms, but it's about focus. When it comes to you and your goals, make sure you focus your energy on challenges that are worth the battle.

As you step into your lead role in the spotlight in those first few years of practice, the greatest tool is to never forget who you are—that's what will truly remind you to be humble and show respect and kindness to everyone from your teammates to your patient. It will also ensure that you maintain your self-respect in the face of negativity, giving you a solid foundation from which to deal with obstacles and problems within your team.

In this, practice makes progress, and I look at it as another tool to perfect—the same way I have to fine-tune my use of tenotomies and how to suture more quickly and effectively. Perfection is a wonderful goal to aim for, but a permanent, honed skill makes more of an impact...and that only comes with progressive application and implementation. So I spend hours of time practicing those skills. During those first few years, I learned how to perform surgery through a smaller incision—and when you take what would normally be a ten centimeter incision down to three centimeters, you know you're honing your craft. Similarly, future adversities will seem like a mere molehill to crush, rather than an insurmountable mountain you have to climb.

I won't lie; the knowledge that you are doing something important doesn't make it hurt less when you come up against sabotage and disrespect, especially when that negativity is due to aspects of your identity. You can use that hurt, however, to make yourself better as a person and as a leader—if you find new ways to channel it, I can guarantee that it will build you up instead of tearing you down.

That is what will make you not only a leader but a shareholder in your chosen field, and in turn, that status will ensure that you have the leverage to be an advocate for others like you. There will always be times when you'll have to fight on their behalf, but as a shareholder, you will have the ability to remove obstacles from their path, just as others have done for you.

DR. BILBREW: THE UNICORN SHAREHOLDER

Being a shareholder at Resurgens Orthopaedic means that I have an equal partnership with the other shareholders in the company. Once I was able to produce my own salary as a surgeon, with my practice operating in the black (financially net-positive), and had passed my Orthopaedic Oral and Written Board Examinations, I was nominated and then voted in as shareholder. I was able to accomplish this in less than the two years required of employed physicians at the time. Because of this, I am no longer simply employed at Resurgens; I have a vote and a financial stake in the company, as well as a certain amount of protection.

I am the first and, at the time of this writing, the only Black woman orthopaedic surgeon to be a shareholder at Resurgens. I know that makes me something of a unicorn, being a Black woman, an immigrant, in a position of power in a White, male-dominated field in America. Despite my status, I still see other would-be unicorns from similar backgrounds who are still struggling in their journeys, so I can't feel yet that I have *made it*.

For instance, I have spoken about microaggressions and outright misogynist and racist treatment:

Yes, I have been mistaken for the janitor or the delivery person when I'm at the hospital. More times than I can count.

Yes, I have been called "Lattisha LaToyah" like it is a clownish, ethnic name rather than something of which I am proud.

Yes, I have been belittled for the way I dress, and my personal style has been criticized for being too colorful and too flashy.

All these actions are attempts—sometimes ignorant, other times deliberate—to put me in my place as a Black woman occupying space in a majority world. They are meant to belittle me and my accomplishments. And these kinds of actions aren't past tense for me. Even as a practicing physician and partner in my company, I am still faced with aggressions and scrutiny that are not based on how I perform my job but on how I look, the pigmentation of my skin, and my gender.

When you are representing a small group, you hold the weight of that on your shoulders—and just because you *can* hold that weight doesn't mean it isn't a heavy load. You bear that burden not just mentally and emotionally, but physically at times, always striving to show the world the best possible version of yourself ...as a constant representation of people who look like you.

I have borne, and continue to bear, this weight to the best of my ability; however, what truly bothers me is watching how my mentees continue to struggle within the system.

Recently, I have been working with a group of Black orthopaedic surgeons in order to take action on behalf of our mentees. We are collecting and presenting research showing clearly that Black residents are being fired from their training programs at a much higher rate than their White male counterparts.

I have also been helping one of my mentees, the first Black female resident at a prestigious program, who is being harassed by the other residents. They call her overexaggerated, African-American ethnic names and have put the hands of cadavers in her afro—among other things. These are not simple, good-natured jokes on the new girl. These are blatant acts of aggression against a Black woman. Other orthopaedic programs have fired Black residents during their first year of training, after placing them on probation within months of starting the program. This is previously unheard of; an intern year is created to train and provide grace, oversight, and mentorship. It is meant to encourage, discipline, and teach, but instead mentees are left depressed, despondent, and unprepared.

Those barriers and obstacles are heavy, but that's why we have to pick them up and carry them out of the way of our mentees—and figure out how to help these future physicians climb over them. We need to give them every chance of getting through the training process based on their merits, regardless of the color of their skin, their gender, their orientation, and more. My goal is not to be the only one like me in the room, but to have a room that represents the world we live in—because when that room doesn't represent society, it's going to continually discourage people who aren't White cishet men from trying to enter. *It is our duty to persevere and instill that perseverance in each upcoming generation.*

Therefore, I can never just sit back and merely enjoy my shareholder status; because of that status, I now need to take my turn to build a foundation and lift up others like me. I have to be an opportunity creator, participating in mentoring programs, being on women-in-medicine panels, joining boards of directors, hosting students who are job-shadowing, and more.

When I have interns and mentees who are literally scared to finish their training because of the way they are being treated by their peers and their supervisors, I have to be the one who shows up and speaks up for them. I am that mentor who will make a special trip to sit in the back of the room, waiting until whoever is responsible walks my way. Then, as politely as possible but while staring that person dead in the eyes, I will explain why they can't treat my mentee differently than all the rest. I have been known to speak directly: *Jim, what the hell is going on in your program? Why are you letting people target my mentees?*

I'm not the only one who feels this way; in fact, there are several other unicorns like me in the medical field who feel like it is part of our job to stand for the underrepresented and the voiceless because we have all been there. We have all felt like our voice has been taken away at one point or another, and because we had people like Dr. Simpson-Mason and Dr. Dell who fought for us and raised their voices to help us, we are committed to doing the same for as long as it takes.

Unfortunately, when we point out discrepancies and aggressions, we are often told we are overreacting or being overly sensitive. That's when we have to dig down into ourselves for the strength to speak out more firmly and stand our ground—and we also have to make sure we have documented facts and examples as evidence.

When the room is representative of true diversity, my fellow unicorns and I will be able to relax. Until then, we will stay vigilant.

EVERY CASE IS THE FIRST CASE

Another reason I know I still haven't *made it*? Despite my shareholder status, I still have plenty to lose, and just like many other Black professionals, I have to continue to work hard in order to keep proving myself worthy of my position.

While my shareholder status means I have a certain amount of safety when it comes to my position at Resurgens, that doesn't mean I am untouchable. I may own a part of the company, but I am aware that everything I have could be taken away in the blink of an eye. If I get injured or ill to the point I can't operate, or if something happens to the company, I won't have a job. I saw this clearly during the COVID-19 pandemic, a time in the world where no one took anything for granted.

We never know what is going to happen tomorrow, so we have to stay humble, and we have to keep working like it means something to us, because it does. I am still considered an early-career surgeon when compared to most of my colleagues, so it's on me to find ways to improve and to refine my tools and skills. *Practice, reinforce, practice, reinforce.* You should never stop learning, because no doctor knows everything, no matter how many years are under their belt; I feel fortunate every time I can add something new to my tool box.

This applies to interactions with patients too. Staying humble with patients means listening to them and learning from them, because I know better than to be cocky and condescending with the people I am trying to help.

If I don't see anything wrong in an X-ray but my patient insists, "I don't know what's going on, but it just doesn't feel right, Doc," I listen to them. I have a wealth of medical knowledge and plenty of diagnostic methodology, but the patient knows their body best. If I ignore their pain and their instincts, I'm not their doctor anymore—I'm just some arrogant woman in a white coat giving them medicine to take without telling them what it's for, and making them feel lesser-than in the process.

We can stay humble and practice humility without losing who we are or decreasing ourselves. I am still very much Dr. Bilbrew, and I'm very proud of myself and what I can do, but I'm not going to make myself or my ego more important than my patients' needs. When something is wrong but I can't find it, I tell my patients the truth; I am humble enough to recognize when I can't fix something, so I say outright, "I'm going to get a second set of eyes on it. If I can't fix what's wrong, we'll find someone who can." Other times, the simple encouragement of, "Just because the X-ray or MRI does not show an abnormality, that does not disqualify your pain. Let's keep searching until we find a solution."

The easiest thing to do when you think you're on top—when you think you've *made it*—is to forget where you came from, to forget that you were once an intern who didn't know shit about shit and *knew* you didn't know shit about shit. When you assume you know everything, have seen everything, and can do everything, you are setting yourself up to make major mistakes to the detriment of your patients' well-being and your career.

I wish more physicians kept in touch with their inner intern, because patient care would be a very different environment. There would be more compassion when sharing diagnoses, more empathy, and more sincerity toward the people who need our help. I never want to lose that humility and that ability to serve my patients well, so I strive to remember to take the time and the care to treat every case like it's my first case.

LESSON

Never lose touch with your inner intern.

FAITH AND TRUST (AND BALANCE)

When I look at the life I have created for myself, I am grateful for everything I have and for the fact that, despite having a busy schedule—I am not burned out. I have some friends who burned out in medical school, while others burned out in residency or during their first years in practice, but I'm still going strong. I look forward to going to work every day and being in the OR. I welcome every chance to help my patients and my mentees. And I do my best to stay fluid and adaptable through balance and trust.

I have managed to prioritize balance between my home life and my work life. There are times when work has to be more of a priority, and other times when family has to be the priority. You have to be ready to shift and readjust when the situation calls for it, sometimes in the moment and sometimes for a prolonged period of time.

You can only maintain the balance you need when you set and uphold boundaries. Early in my career, I set boundaries and stuck to them, adapting them as necessary in order to maintain the balance. Those boundaries may be different at different stages of your life and career, but when they are in place, it's crucial that you view them as hard lines that cannot be crossed.

For instance, maybe you want to be home by a certain time four days a week, 80 percent of the time. That becomes a boundary, so any time you are approached with something that might impinge upon that boundary, you have to make a decision—is it important enough to be part of the 20 percent where you make an allowance? Is it the kind of emergency worth keeping you in the clinic or the OR until 10:00 p.m. when you're trying to be home by 6:00 p.m.? What and who is worth smudging the lines of your boundaries? That requires an understanding of your priorities, importance, and time. It is an advanced skill set that is acquired through the loss of opportunity as well as the acquisition of quality experiences to determine who and what is able to breach your set boundaries in that 20-percent leeway.

There are also times when you should allow little-to-no wiggle room to cross boundaries. For instance, when it comes to how people speak to you, or treat you, there should be no *20 percent* of leeway. You have to clearly define for yourself what you will and will not allow—and you have to stick to that boundary. When something crosses over, you have to address it and shut it down.

There will always be situations that are out of your control, even though you have boundaries in place. If you find yourself out of control more often than you are in control, you are out of balance. Your priorities will be, too, and the balanced life you create will slowly fall apart.

When it comes to trust and creating the life you want, you also have to find the object/person/vision/goal that you can trust in, beyond all doubt. *Trust* can be defined in many ways, but for me, it's something that keeps me grounded and gives me peace at all points in my life. When someone or something continually and persistently destroys that trust, I precisely and ultimately remove that source from my life.

Some people place their trust primarily in themselves and their abilities. For others, they trust someone close to them, like a spouse or a partner. For me, it's God. I have always been a faith-based person, and my spiritual roots run deep, all the way back through my earliest childhood in Handsworth. My faith in God makes me feel supported and strong, and He is always with me; it is something I can always trust, regardless of any white noise in the background.

If you don't have something to trust that brings you this kind of certainty, you run the risk of becoming prematurely burned out. Life's rocky roads are just too difficult to navigate without having something to aid in your stability; eventually, you'll lose your way. Identify what or who you can trust in, whether that is a person, a deity, or the simple idea of what you will one day become or accomplish, but above all, trust in something, if not yourself.

SHARE THE WEALTH

For me, being a shareholder goes far beyond just the financial investment and security I have found in my professional life. Yes, it gives me a little more reason to puff my chest and a little more reason to hold my head high, but it also brings a philosophy of change and a call to action: now that I have the status, the finances, and the title, what can I do with them?

As you attain status, power, and ultimately, privilege, people are always going to be looking up to you and needing your help to climb a little higher on their own personal journey. The ability to extend a hand and help them up should be a major part of what drives you to continually succeed—and while I still feel I have yet to *make it*, I can and do use my power and privilege on behalf of others, to inspire them not only to meet me as we journey to the top, but to potentially surpass me.

Humility goes hand-in-hand with this and all endeavors. Don't forget your true reasons for pursuing and attaining your goal.

LESSON

Whatever drives you will keep you ethical and empathetic. It will allow you to be a better person, a better leader, and a better physician.

Remember your purpose and your origin story—those two north stars will help keep you humble. I am just one generation removed from cleaning hospital floors, and that knowledge always keeps me in check when I start to think I'm above it all.

As you adapt to and maneuver within any new personal or professional paradigm, keep close to your core values, but remain open and flexible. Define what is most important to you and make sure you're not changing those aspects of your character and personality as you adapt to the world around you—and don't be afraid to scale new heights whenever possible; you are simply building the platform that will serve as the foundation for the generation after yours.

Call to Action

I learned the importance of enjoying life and taking time for myself from Dr. Dell, but even after coming through my first five years successfully, I have never gotten so comfortable with my accomplishments and my position in life to the point I feel I can coast for a while. This can be a difficult concept to accept at times, but I firmly believe if you value yourself and your goals in life, you cannot rest on your laurels for too long.

You can—and should be—proud of everything you accomplish, but the world can be a harsh place, and it doesn't care how accomplished you are. This is why it's so important to maintain your humility and compassion, too. If you are coming to your journey from an unprivileged place in life, chances are it is going to be twice as hard for you to accomplish that journey than it will be for others, and even once you reach your goal, you'll have to work twice as hard to maintain your position. You can't stop being meticulous—not until we reach true equality.

You don't have the luxury to put your feet up and say, *Well, I've made it.* Why? Because someone out there is waiting for you to make a mistake. Someone else out there wants the job you have, and they aren't resting. They're working, learning, and waiting. Show them *daily*, through your work ethic and grit, why you have earned the position you're in.

I take this philosophy to heart. I can't say I'm too tired to bring in a student to job-shadow me. It's not an option. When a surgical society emails me to say, "Dr. Bilbrew, we'd love to have you on our board of directors," I can't just email back and tell them I'm too busy. I have thought about it, of course—how easy it would be to just write a note and explain all my excuses: *I'm exhausted. I'm writing a book. I'm starting a fashion line. I'm going through personal issues.*

Nope. If they need me on the board, I am going to be on that board. The instant I voice any such complaints as a young surgeon with only a few years of practice under my belt, I am going to hear those other senior surgeons come right back at me: *"I'm sixty years old. I have been doing this for thirty years. You are allowed to rest, but you must always persevere!"*

Regardless of what I have accomplished, and what Black women like me have accomplished, I know society hasn't shifted yet. What we are doing is a drop in the ocean of change, which isn't to say that it's not significant. In 1920, women gained the right to vote, but except for a few significant outliers, women weren't accepted at most medical schools at that time, much less women of color.

If one time traveler from 1848 and one from 1948 showed up in my OR, they would both be astounded to see someone who looks like me holding the scalpel.

Society has changed quite a bit since then, but the last time I was asked if I was the *actual* doctor or the hospital janitor who was supposed to clean the OR was 2022—so it hasn't changed enough.

I once heard an older Black female physician stand in front of a room of majority White males to speak on her journey in medicine. She described the constant barrage of micro- and macroaggressions as a death by a thousand cuts. I sympathized with her; she was tired, exhausted, and fed up. She had reached her thousandth cut, and yet was still pushing forward, and doing so courageously.

Courage, stamina, grit. That's what it takes to keep going. Even better: don't wait for that thousandth cut to bleed out. Take these lessons and suture yourself up; stop and rest; and get a blood transfusion from friends, family, colleagues in the form of inspiration if you have to, but *never give up*. As my grandfather would say, "Never give up, never look back too long, and always move forward."

12

CLIMB EVERY MOUNTAIN

Some people never forget their earliest childhood dreams, despite achieving a huge lifetime goal—even doctors. It may be something based in creativity such as my initial childhood aspirations to be a hairstylist; it may be something that involves seeking adventure, or new life experiences. We all have an inner child tugging on our sleeve to remind us that there are more mountains out there to climb.

I am not the only one who feels this way—I've seen other physicians find new avenues for expression and fulfillment while maintaining their primary careers. One of my friends is a pediatrician, for example, but she always dreamed about becoming an entrepreneur. Today, while running a successful pediatric practice, she also teaches thousands of other physicians how to build profitable businesses so they can live life and practice medicine on their own terms. Success on your path doesn't have to exclude other dreams; it just means you have to learn how to balance your responsibilities in order to pursue them, as well.

In my first five years as a surgeon, I was fully focused on my practice and my family, but once I became a shareholder, I began looking around me and inside myself for new goals to pursue. One of them is this book, while the other is a bit more personal, something of which my creative inner child would definitely approve.

Creativity is part of my heritage. Despite their careers taking them out of that world professionally, both of my parents are creative people and artists at heart, so I grew up in an environment that encouraged artistic expression. My mother majored in fashion and textiles and my dad attended art school. As a result, young Lattisha was encouraged to find her own sense of style and consequently loved to express herself in different originative outlets. From those humble beginnings, however, I developed a lifelong love of creativity that I have kept alive in little ways, such as my ability to pull in a sense of fashion into my daily clinic outfits. While at one point in my training I was admonished for my style, now I adorn myself in colorful, unique ways as an expression of my personality and my heritage.

Surgery, however, is not the typical field for wearing fashion-forward and vibrant outfits. Doctors and nurses are generally expected to dress conservatively, even in terms of the colors and patterns of their scrubs. It's been intensely frustrating for me, especially as a Black woman who too often gets mistaken for a janitor or an orderly when wearing bland, shapeless scrubs.

When you are going through surgical training, you're taught that you either wear hospital scrubs or dress professionally to clinics—meaning a black, blue, or gray suit and white shirt, or its equivalent. I was made fun of and even chastised during my residency because of the way I dressed; my bright colors and unique accessories were too much for the conservative sensibilities of orthopaedics. During the rest of my time in training, I heeded those casual warnings to an extent, but I was really only biding my time.

As a practicing surgeon, I indulge my love of wearing bright colors and accessorizing. By doing so, I normalized my sense of fashion in the clinic and operating room; consequently, it has become a part of my brand and who I am as a surgeon. I turned the negative remarks from residency about my style of dress and fashion sense into one of the cornerstones of how I represent myself as a practicing orthopaedic surgeon.

When going through a training process or a journey, you often have to subdue parts of who you are to survive. Think, act, and react like a chameleon. The survival characteristics of a chameleon stems from its two greatest assets: its ability to adapt, and its ability to focus in two different directions at the same time.

When crossing a treacherous desert, the chameleon does not adorn itself in bright natural hues, to prevent attracting predators. Without changing who you are, you adapt to your surroundings and become a chameleon. The chameleon does not change its ability to manifest a rainbow of colors; it just wisely determines when to show them. It is a survival tactic, when immersed in environments that are foreign, or even hostile. Just like the chameleon once it's back safely in its own environment, you adorn all the colors of who you are.

Chameleons are also the only lizards who can see in two different directions at once. They can maintain concentration, direction, and focus on two separate images. In the same manner, you are more than your title; you can be a physician and a fashion designer, a physician and an entrepreneur, a physician and... fill in the blank.

After all these years, I have achieved my primary goal in life and have found fulfillment in being an orthopaedic surgeon, but I never forgot that little girl who also loved to express herself creatively. My passion for fashion is combined with a kind of restlessness, that feeling that I need a new challenge. I looked within and focused on the artistic side that has always been intrinsic to me, and I remembered that wide-eyed little girl full of creativity and wonder. Now that I was in a position to put my stamp on another achievement, I realized that I never wanted to lose that part of myself—and the best way to keep my inner child close was to see those creative dreams come to fruition.

While continuing to progress and grow my thriving surgical career, I'm embarking on a new venture I have wanted to tackle for a long time: launching a line of designer scrubs for medical professionals. Putting my money where my mouth is—and where my dreams have been—I have launched Windrush and Co., a line of fashion scrubs that honors my family's style and sensibilities by adopting that sense of sophistication, confidence, and refinement. I will also be able to honor my grandparents and their journey from Jamaica by adopting their generation's moniker for my business. This seems like a fitting way to come full circle, bringing my heritage proudly to the forefront in every way, because none of this would have been possible for me without the foundation they provided all those decades ago.

Like the chameleon, I have had my time for adaptation, and now I can focus on climbing a new mountain. Don't ignore those things that call you to challenge yourself and attempt new outlets and goals, whether that is tapping into your creativity or an interest you've had since you were a small child. Climb those mountains; remember your dreams; create and conquer new goals.

LESSON

Always find something new to pursue. Refocus the lens through which you analyze your life, and you will always find a new goal to aspire to.

YES, I CAN . . .

When I began actively working to make Windrush and Co. a reality, I heard from both my supporters and detractors. From my parents and other allies, there were thoughtful questions, offers of advice, and clear statements of support. From my detractors, I heard skepticism in questions like *Can you do that?* and *Do you have time for that?* I dealt with those questions as politely and patiently as possible—using that filter of kindness again—but I also did not let those questions phase me, because the answers to those two questions are simple: *yes* and *yes*.

I don't allow other people to have a voice in what my goals should be or how I should achieve them. When I figure out what I want to do, I make that personal drive my focus, and I don't let the white noise distract me along the way.

LESSON

We don't strive to accomplish goals to please our critics.

Am I nervous about putting myself out there in a whole different capacity as a fashion designer? *Yes.*

Am I afraid this new endeavor might fail? *Of course.*

Am I procrastinating here and there? *Absolutely.*

Am I letting fear stop me from doing my best to make it a success? *Hell, no.* I'm embracing this new energy rising up in me while I prepare to conquer this mountain.

I am excited about the chance to tap into a new facet of myself and increase my self-awareness—no matter the outcome. I am trusting in the toolbox I have been using my entire life to help me adapt and maneuver as I scale this new height—and I'm trusting in the support and encouragement of the people who love me and want me to succeed.

I am also hoping that this new trail I'm blazing will broaden the horizons even more for the people coming up behind me. I want to be an example that we can do anything we set our minds to, regardless of how we are labeled or what society tells us.

...AND SO CAN YOU

How do you know you're ready to scale new heights? The simplest way to know is to try, because the truth is, you'll never know if you're ready until you do it. Like my parents told me when I was hesitant to start any new goal: *if it doesn't scare you, it's not big enough.*

You can't just wait around for acknowledgment; it's up to you to make it happen. No one is going to push you across the finish line; no one will be able to look inside your mind and write down that business idea. You are capable, you are equipped, and you can do it. Look at me—I'm an orthopaedic surgeon who is also a mother, an author, and a fashion designer, and I claim all of those labels proudly. Every single one of those accomplishments scared me along the way at one point or another, but I've kept going and trusted in myself, God, and my tool box.

They all scared me, and in a way, that's why I had to tackle them. Any time I hesitated or questioned myself, I remembered what Dr. Mason told me all those years ago: *Piss or get off the pot, Lattisha.* I made my choices, and I've never looked back. Remember, nothing worth having in life is easy. Think of your passion in life—along with your goals and dreams—as a muscle you are building in the gym. The only way you know if you have truly worked that muscle enough to build and shape it is when it gets a little sore after the workout. That is when you see gains.

You are more than just your title; you are the culmination of your journey and life story. Therefore, it's dangerous to allow what we do for a living to define who we are; that mindset makes it easier to close ourselves off from new opportunities and new passions. If you maintain enough balance, you'll be able to take pride in your professional accomplishments without becoming arrogant or complacent, and you'll be ready and able to find new challenges and scale new heights that will teach you even more about yourself.

If you're on a journey right now and you're trying to accomplish something, don't settle for less. Don't be afraid to take on new challenges, but don't be afraid to turn down ones that aren't intrinsic to you and your life. Climb those mountains that call to you, whether they appeal to your inner child or your adult self; ideally, both parts of you will find fulfillment along the way.

Pay attention to the lessons you've learned, and understand and accept that you're going to doubt yourself at times, no matter how much trust you've placed in yourself and your skills. Make your decision to piss or get off the pot. And once you make that decision, don't question it or allow criticisms to distract you from achieving your goals.

Part of our responsibility is to push forward and to keep working for something greater, not just for the betterment of the world but for ourselves. And that toolbox you've been building? It's bottomless. It's never ending. You can fill it up with whatever you want, with every tool you've ever needed, and there's going to be a purpose for everything in there, from the simplest tool to the most complex.

There's always going to be a new tool and a new way to use it, just like there's always going to be a purpose and a use for you beyond your job title. Never doubt that.

CONCLUSION

"How am I even going to study for my fracture conference when they've got me so anxious, Dr. Bilbrew?" she asked me over the phone.

One of my mentees, a Black woman, has been struggling in her intern year, and she's dealing with aggression and emotional stress while she's trying to keep up with her work—the kind of situation in which it feels like you are being set up to fail.

"They're trying to set me up to be seen as this difficult resident," she concluded, her voice sounding so defeated.

"Number one, stop what you're doing," I said. "Just pause right here. Now, assign yourself a time and place for relaxation."

I suggested she take forty-five minutes and do whatever relaxes her, then to come back to it and study when she was feeling more positive. "You'll be okay," I finished.

She agreed, but before we got off the phone, she asked quietly, "How do I go through another five years of this?"

I had to take a minute before I could answer her, because the question took my breath away for a moment. "Honey," I said, gently. "It's not five years. This is a lifetime we're talking about. It's not just residency or your fellowship."

Silence on the other end of the phone.

"I deal with the same things you deal with, and it's been over a decade since I started residency. It may never get any easier," I said. "Are you still going to run this race? Because we need you here."

It's true. We need people like her in orthopaedics and other spaces like it, because there are people out there who need her to succeed. She hasn't met them yet, but they are her future patients, her future mentees, her future children—all the people who will be directly and indirectly affected by her choice to work in that field.

And I believe that she can get there and achieve her goals, no matter how hard it gets, because she can use all those tools we've already talked about. They are already inside her, and she can refine them and find new uses for them. But most importantly, she has to keep going, she must persevere—and so must you.

LEVERAGE YOUR TOOLS

One of my favorite quotes is from Archimedes: "Give me a lever long enough and a fulcrum on which to place it, and I shall move the world." I think of my grandparents and my parents when I read that quote, and I think of other people who have inspired me—people who have had the inner strength as a fulcrum to move the world when they needed to.

To put this quote in the perspective of everything I have talked about in this book: Your ability to be the only one like you in the room is the lever, and the social perception of a minority in a majority environment is the placement. *You* are the fulcrum—and that gives you the power and privilege to change the world.

At this point in your journey, you've been assembling your toolbox and adding tools, and you are in a position of strategy no matter where you are along the way. For instance, as a shareholder and a practicing surgeon, I am in a position of influence and power over fellows, residents, and medical students alike. If you are a fellow, you are in a position of influence and power over residents; if you are an intern, you are in a position of influence and power over medical students.

If you strategize, you can use your influence and authority to be a source of inspiration to those who look up to you. In order to do this, there are a few things to prioritize:

1. **You have to persevere.** You have to make the decision to be on this journey and to continue it, even when it becomes difficult.

2. **You have to stay positive**, even when you don't feel positive about certain elements of the journey.

3. **You have to be vulnerable** and share the failures as well as the successes of your own journey.

4. **You have to be open** to giving help and receiving help—even if you don't find it easy to seek assistance.

In order to stay on track to achieve your goals, you have to keep your planned outcome in focus and be honest with yourself about what you can achieve. Remember what is pushing you to keep going and persevere, because that is what will bring out the warrior in you along the way. Knowing who you are and what you can do will ensure that you have the best possible leverage with which to move the world.

ASSEMBLING THE TOOLBOX

Throughout this book, I have discussed psychological tools I have picked up along my journey to becoming an orthopaedic surgeon—a journey that began in my Nanny's hospital room in England and has brought me to a position of power and privilege as a shareholder and board-certified orthopaedic surgeon in my practice.

I highlighted many of these tools within the preceding chapters, and these are among the most important:

- → **Find your steady in-between.** Within you is a worrier-warrior and a patient perseverer. The sooner you find the best way for you to balance between them, the more time you will have to practice using this tool. If you can find your balance and adjust it as you need, you'll be able to maintain and use both aspects of your personality during the most difficult points of your life.
- → **Never settle. You can do better.** There is an important difference between settling and compromising. When you settle, you make do with less—and that may mean not meeting your goal or losing resources that could help you reach your goal. Compromise means accepting changes along your journey as accepting one thing in exchange for another but still arriving at the same goal.
- → **Self-awareness comes from challenges, successes, and failures alike.** You will learn important aspects of who you are from all three of these elements. The challenges you choose to accept will show you what is both intrinsic to you and what is important to you. Meanwhile,

your successes and failures alike can be used as a platform of educational experiences, if you learn from them.

- **Let others tell you *no*; don't say it to yourself.** When someone else tells you *no*, you can view that as a starting point. If you're in a race, they may tell you not to run it or hide your shoes to make it more difficult for you, but you can still overcome that negativity. However, if you tell yourself *no*, you've chopped your feet off before the race even starts. Setting boundaries is important, but so is keeping yourself from self-negation; it's the difference between *I won't* (boundaries) and *I can't* (self-negation).

- **Push forward.** Having the strength to push forward despite obstacles and negativity is crucial to your journey. It will give you consistency and motivation even when you can't feel like you can achieve your goals; perseverance is a muscle, and it must be built up and maintained through action rather than emotion. When you focus on the end goal, it's easier to keep the perspective you'll need to keep going.

- **Eliminate the negative by any means necessary.** Negativity from others is unavoidable when you are on a difficult journey, but you cannot allow it to continue or build up inside you like a cancer. Sometimes you can avoid or confront negativity without metaphorical bloodshed, but there are times when you simply have to take decisive action to cut negativity out quickly and cleanly. And just as in surgery, the best tool for that is one that is razor-sharp.

→ **Find those who believe in you and understand you.** Finding people who believe in you is crucial to achieving your goals, whether those people function as supporters, mentors, or sponsors along your journey. It's especially important to find those people who not only want you to succeed but also understand your journey; while your family may love you and hold you up to their best ability, the people you can trust within your field of study are just as important. You need people who understand you and your journey in order to have your best chance to strategize and level up in your training and your career.

→ **Embrace leadership, but establish boundaries.** When you're part of a professional team, you'll have more authority and more connections to juggle than ever before. Remember to maintain your filters of kindness, authority, and humility when interacting with the people on your team, but also set your own boundaries in order to maintain professional relationships and ensure that you are treated with respect.

- → **Don't make life harder for others or allow others to do that to you.** Life is short; there's no reason to make life harder for anyone or to allow anyone else to make it harder for you. As a leader, you should strive to foster an environment of kindness and show up for your team, even if you've been subject to unkind environments in the past. When you are the only one in the room, you have to advocate for others in order to be a true team player; allowing yourself to be dormant means allowing yourself to become a doormat.
- → **Trust in your own style.** You may worry about being set apart or standing out from the crowd because of who you are or how you do things, but those elements of your character are important in how you will distinguish yourself. It's not enough to simply overcome life's challenges; it's *how* you overcome them that helps you define your personal style. When you're on stage, everyone will be looking to see how you perform, so be ready to show them who you are.
- → **Be adaptable and open to new challenges.** We always have to adapt and change along our path to success, but we also have to do that when we achieve our primary goals. If you are fluid and open to new challenges and new opportunities, you'll utilize all aspects of yourself in new and exciting ways—keeping yourself at less risk

of burnout or stagnation. You are always capable of more in life, and finding new mountains to climb and new trails to blaze will ensure that you maintain your balance and stay fulfilled.

→ **Stay humble.** Never forget who you are, and where you came from—and how much work it's taken to get you where you are today. If you treat every patient or team member the way you would like to be treated and approach every new case like it's your first one, you'll maintain the perspective you need to be your best self.

When I decided to write this book, I knew that I wanted to use the illustration of the toolbox as one of the central concepts; I also knew I wanted to make identifying and defining specific tools an ongoing theme. With that in mind, I also knew that the toolbox I was addressing throughout the book wasn't *my* toolbox, but *yours*.

GET MOVING

This book was never meant to teach you who you are—you already know that. It was never meant to help you build a toolbox—you already have one. My goal was to help you make that toolbox shine and to help you stock it full of useful tools for your journey in life.

Whatever the state of your psychological toolbox when you started the book—whether it was just dusty and in need of a good polish, or it was fragile, damaged, and in need of serious repair—I hope you now have a truly gorgeous toolbox, one that reflects your personal style and that you can rely on and be proud of.

How you use your toolbox and the tools inside it are up to you, but I sure would love to hear about what you're building. Reach out to me at drlattishabilbrew.com or email me at info@drlattisha bilbrew.com.

You're the fulcrum. You're holding the lever, and you've been given the opportunity to stand.

It's time to move the world.

CPSIA information can be obtained
at www.ICGtesting.com
Printed in the USA
BVHW041642200323
660796BV00010B/111/J